Gamachu & Mindfulness

A Physician's Journey

From Bako (Ethiopia) to the Bronx, New York

The **Past** is memory,

but I believe in the power of **Now!**

By

Zergabachew Asfaw, M.D. FACP

Copyright © 2023

All Rights Reserved

ISBN: 978-1088231012

All rights reserved. No part of this publication may be reproduced, distributed, or transmitted in any form or by any means, including photocopying, recording, or other electronic or mechanical methods, without the author's prior written permission, except in the case of brief quotations embodied in critical reviews and certain other non-commercial uses permitted by copyright law. For permission requests, please get in touch with the author.

Table of Contents

Dedication and Acknowledgments i
Preface 1
Introduction 2
Chapter 1: The King Has a Great Fall 8
Chapter 2: Plucked from the Forest 28
Chapter 3: Crossing Hao Janjero's River 41
Chapter 4: Choosing Doubt over Dogma 54
Chapter 5: A Rift so Deep 67
Chapter 6: 'Blood that Freezes, Blood that Burns' 82
Chapter 7: Asking Until I Got the Answer 98
Chapter 8: A Year of Thirteen Months 111
Chapter 9: Gamachu 122
Chapter 10: Hale Luya 133
Chapter 11: My Father's Shade 143
Chapter 12: The Pull of Politics 155
Chapter 13: My Teachers, My Patients 170
Chapter 14: The Heart of Lightness 181
Chapter 15: Mindfulness is What Matters Most 194
Conclusion 203

Dedication and Acknowledgments

This book is dedicated to individuals who have influenced me over several years. The list is very long, and the range of time is wide- from childhood to senior years. Every human being has a circle of influence, whether it is negative or positive.

My grandmother Elmitu Boru forced me to stay under the shade of the tree with my private instructor (Aba Basho), who taught me how to read Geez for the first time. The first language that I learned was the Oromo language. My instructor was a priest from the Ethiopian Orthodox church. Elmitu Boru was revered by her community and loved by her children. Her husband, Fitawrari Gamachu Moticha, was killed during the local conflict after returning from Maychew, where he confronted invading Italian army along with other Ethiopian patriots. His brother Kuru Moticha was killed at the battle at Maychew while defending his country from the invading Italian army. I was told that my grandfather was preparing for guerilla warfare against the invading Italian army. My father, Asfaw Gamachu, and my stepmother Tigist Bezou led me to modern education. My father is instrumental in establishing several schools in his home village Tulumara and other regions. He was a lifelong fighter to promote education among his people. His younger brother Aknaw Gamachu was a critical thinker in the family.

I used to discuss several topics with him, including religion, law, and politics, during my formative years. He had served in the Ethiopian parliament during Emperor Haile Selassie's era.

My stepmother, Tigist Bezou, gave me unconditional love and encouragement. My cousin, Dessalegn Amanu, is an exemplary in search of knowledge.

I have numerous friends and teachers who have helped me to see the world from different angles. Dr Ambachew Worreta, Dr Abebe Haregewoin, Dr Wondossen Gebre, Dr Efrem Alemayehu, Dr Seifu Daniel, Dr Wonduwosen Tadesse, Dr Fassil Tefera, Professor Tilahun Adera, professor Awash Teklehaimanot, Dr Owen. L. Wood and Nega Seyoum are a few long-time friends who influenced me. Professor Taye Makuria, Professor Edemariam Tsega, Professor Bayou Teklu, and professor Eyassu H. Gaber are some of my teachers and friends who impacted my thoughts. Dr. Owen L. Wood was my mentor and friend who introduced me to virology research and helped me connect with professor Robert E. Shope of Yale University to work on arboviruses. Dr. Bisrat Aklilu persuaded me to publish my memoir when I told him what I had gone through in Axum, Tigray region of Ethiopia, as a young doctor. I would like to extend my gratitude and appreciation to my longtime friend professor Haregewoin Asefa for her honesty and sincerity in sharing and discussing several topics of major importance in today's world. My gratitude is extended to many thinkers who have influenced me in the pursuit of knowledge and the truth.

Capitain Kebede Woldetsadik who is a lifelong friend and helped me to know more about Ethiopian Airline and whose curiosity about medicine inspired me, has been very supportive to me all the time. Kibebe Tsehai is also another lifelong friend whose views are indispensable.

Preface

I initially wanted to name this book, *when the nomad stands still,* but I changed the title because I have to be joyful about life. Many of us take for granted all the good things that we have and the experiences we go through. I named the book ,*Gamachu,* which means Joy or happiness in the Oromo language (the largest ethnic group in Ethiopia). My grandfather's name is Gamachu.

In the summer of 2001, I picked up my father, Asfaw Gamachu, from Newark International Airport when he came to visit me. The joy that I noted on his face when he saw me was great, and so was mine. He expressed his appreciation of this land, as I was driving him toward my residence in Pomona, NY. Gamachu is the name I gave to my son, who is twenty-five years old now, and we have both lived in Pomona ever since he was born. I changed the original title of my memoir because of the joyful moments that I have observed among multitudes of Ethiopians as a result of the positive transformations that took place under the leadership of Dr. Abiy Ahmed. This was the feeling that many people shared when the popular movement for change, started a few years ago. Change is difficult, but it is inevitable. I was not sure how long that joy could last among people. How can we get a lasting joy in life? That is what mindfulness is all about.

Introduction

I wrote this memoir more than fifteen years ago, and I did not have a clear intention to publish it. The year 2018 was a sobering year due to the sweeping change toward democracy as a result of popular upheaval in Ethiopia, under the leadership of Lemma Magarsa, Dr. Abiye Ahmed, Degu Andargachew, and Demeke Makonnen, to mention names of individuals, who were widely recognized by Ethiopians at that time. I have no concern about the merit each one carries. But, my intention is to reflect back on my life and look into the long journey I made.

My formative childhood years were very exciting in many ways. Like many Ethiopian children who were brought up in a village, I was very close to nature. Along with other children of my age, I was a shepherd, but not full-time, and spent days looking for wild berries and fruits. The forest was dense, and it was easy to get closer to wildlife such as antelopes, monkeys, baboons, tigers, a variety of birds, and others. We had to invent various games to entertain ourselves. Then I had to spend days under the shade of a tree with an Ethiopian Orthodox church priest to learn how to read. That was very boring, and thus I hated it. Then, the family moved to a small town, Bako, where I had to attend a modern school. My father was instrumental in building this school, and he himself was attending evening classes at this school. Then, my life was more structured around passing from one grade to the other, elementary school, high school, college, and medical school. There were ups and downs, and the major disruption happened in the seventies when the revolution broke up. A drastic change took place in Ethiopia, and the whole world was shocked by the execution of sixty-nine Haile Selassie's government officials. Since then, I have had a nomadic and unsettled life for many years. My life was not settled.

On February 17, 2019, I attended a public gathering in New York City organized by ECMA (Ethiopian Community Mutual Association) and Global Alliance-Justice for Ethiopian Cause, to commemorate the 1937 massacre of Addis Ababa residents by fascist Italy. Berhane Tadesse, was one of the organizers who invited me to participate. I gave a short talk on the role of patriotic physicians who fought for justice and human rights. We Physicians in North America have an organization named after Hakim Workneh and Melaka Bayan (Society for International Development), two western-trained pioneer physicians. They both served their country during difficult times in the history of that nation. I very emotional and saddened about human sacrifices that took place. People fight for freedom, justice, and basic human rights all over the world. It is notable that thousands of Addis Ababa residents were killed within three days as a result of an assassination attempt on Graziani, who was the designated colonial ruler of Ethiopia during the invasion. That invasion was part of the second world war.

In 1976 when the military regimen took power by disposing Emperor Haile Selassie, thousands of Ethiopians were massacred by Mengistu Hailemariam's socialist government, which lasted for seventeen years under the banner of so-called revolution. I came to the United States of America during that period of turmoil, in July 1989.

Change is an inevitable phenomenon and is a continuous process in this world. My life has changed a lot. I traveled to Ethiopia ten years after Mengistu's regime was removed from power. Since then, I have traveled many times and have witnessed changing social structures and political turmoil. Meles Zenawi, who replaced the military regime by guerilla warfare, based his power on ethnic politics and the old ideology of divide and rule. The nation was divided based on ethnic boundaries, where there were no boundaries at all. Economic power was shifted towards a few government officials and their associates. A new Ethiopian oligarchy was created. National debt skyrocketed, and larceny and hiding stolen money in foreign countries, including the US, became the norm for a handful of elites. Social injustice, political suppression, and human rights violations resulted in the sweeping change that is currently taking place in Ethiopia.

Prime Minister Abiy Ahmed came to power in 2018 and introduced a raft of reforms aimed at helping Ethiopia transition from an authoritarian state to an inclusive democracy. Accordingly, he made a call for peaceful transformation, and he won the Nobel Peace Prize for peace in 2019. However, he faced major challenges due to ethnic-based political parties or boundaries. The Tigrayan oligarchy, that has amassed enormous wealth unchallenged during 27 years of power, demonstrated anger and resistance from the start. They remained disruptive forces and incited violence stating that the old constitution, which needs reform, was violated. Since Dr. Abiy came to office, stating that he is committed to distributing power more evenly, the Tigrayan's political and economic clout has diminished. Their leaders can also face charges related to human rights and security violations and corruption. The regional election in Tigray, took place on September 9, 2020, in spite of the central government's warning of its illegitimacy. There is no doubt that regional autonomy needs to be respected, but the inclusiveness of other opposition parties was in question.

The change has not been easy, and the fact that the new government became inclusive of all oppositions to build a democratic system resulted in unprecedented social turmoil. Ethnicity, dominated federalism or nationalism. Some politicians raised an ethnic banner. Most of the opposition groups that stood against the Abiy's government were extremists of Oromo, Amhara, and Tigray…. The Tigray regional government continued to prepare for outright war and trained enormous militia and special forces, many of whom were under-aged. On November 24, 2020, the Tigray regional government attacked the Ethiopian northern military brigade by recruiting their ethnic groups within the army. A ruthless massacre took place while those who were non-Tigray were sleeping. Unimaginable atrocities were committed. They possessed the ammunition of the northern division of Ethiopian Defense Forces and declared full-fledged war to come back to power.

That led to national anger, and the Ethiopian army was mobilized within a short period of time and successfully diminished the power of TPLF (Tigray Liberation Front), which was designated as a terrorist group by the Ethiopian parliament. The group that is named "junta" got dispersed within three weeks of operation. Historians will write about those revelations. However, in June 2021, the Ethiopian government declared a unilateral ceasefire due to international pressure to alleviate the humanitarian crisis. The TPLF rebels regrouped and launched a massive attack and invaded Amhara and Afar regions and committed genocide against civil society.

It is a widely accepted notion among Ethiopians that the establishment of ethnic-based regional governments has resulted in conflicts and atrocities among people who, in the past, lived in harmony for hundreds of years. Many youths were brainwashed with fictional stories rather than facts about the history of the nation. All leaders make mistakes, but they have respectable contributions as well. The future of a nation cannot be built on the total condemnation of the past.

Thich Nihat Hanh, a Vietnamese scholar and peace activist writes, "When you ask the question, "who am I?" if you have enough time and concentration- you may find some surprising answers. You may see that you are a continuation of your ancestors. Your parents and your ancestors are fully present in every cell of your body; you are their continuation. You do not have a separate self. If you remove your ancestors and your parents from you, there is no "you" left." But mindfulness is what matters most.

Chapter 1: The King Has a Great Fall

My second-year medical school classmates-Top Yohannes W. Michael, left to right, Tadesse Katila, Lukman Hakim, Tadesse Birhane.

It was 1975, and students had flooded the streets of Addis Ababa. Chaos ruled. The military junta had just stripped Haile Selassie of his power and executed 60 government officials. While the young student protesters were demanding change, no one had expected to see bodies splattered all over the streets of the capital. It was an atmosphere where no one was safe, and everyone was suspect. The king observed what was happening in Ethiopia over the years.

I was a second-year medical student. I had spent many nights in the coffee houses and student hangouts talking and proselytizing about corrupt politicians and blood-thirsty soldiers. Our group of students argued about everything: Haile Selassie, capitalism, Anbessa bus drivers, the new education policy, Socialism, the famine, and the Royal Guards. Much like the student population worldwide, Ethiopian students were rebellious and vocal – but, like our fellow students elsewhere, 99 percent of our rebellious banter was just talked. No one could have anticipated what happened next. There was no risk among university students. Today in 2019, university students kill one another due to ethnic differences. That is appalling.

Yohannes Wolde Michael, a good friend, may have had a premonition. The night before his disappearance, we were having coffee in one of those dark cafes where students tend to gather. Yohannes Wolde Michael was jumpy and nervous – not his usual animated self at all. I knew he was connected to the underground student movement, but I was unaware of the extent of his involvement. In Ethiopia in 1975, everyone knew that some secrets were better left unsaid.

I enjoyed Yohannes Wolde Michael's camaraderie and fine intellect – that alone was enough to sustain our friendship – so I stayed away from the particulars of his life. Still, I sensed a deep unease in him that night. He was sweating profusely, even though the breeze from Entotto Mountain swept through the open windows in the cafe and cooled the lingering customers. Nowadays they talk about beautiful Entotto park that we never imagined.

We talked about initiating a change in the Dreg government – a favorite topic – but my friend was jumpy and irritable, which betrayed his usual confidence and good humor. There was no doubt that he was distracted, and everyone noticed that his eyes continually darted toward the door every time a customer or another student walked in. No matter how we tried to engage our friend, he did not let down his guard. Yohannes's discomfort managed to infect our small group that night. We did not know what was going to happen, but we sensed something serious was in the air. Before I got up to leave that night, Yohannes whispered his concern to Tadesse Berhane, another friend, and me. The medical students were composed of health officers and some military officers who have prior experience in life situations. Abraham Verges, who is currently a professor of medicine at Stamford university school of medicine, was one of our classmates who visited the coffee shop with us after classes regularly. He left the country when the situation got worse. The two military officers, Colonel Befekadu Wedajo and Col. Elias Geleta could understand the situation in total.

Ambachew Worreta was a very close friend of the military officers, and they had their own separate groups.

Yohannes said, "I am going to be questioned. They are looking for me." Like a porcelain figurine from Japan, I knew that one wrong move and my life would be shattered and in pieces on the floor.

I would have been terrified at the prospect of what my friend had told me, except that my medical studies kept me preoccupied. I went home that night to my dormitory at Black Lion's Hospital and poured myself into my books. My studies have always been a refuge – a place where I felt I had a sense of control as well as a deep curiosity. I did not have to think about the troubles when my books were spread in front of me. Books transported me to another world – the world of the mind. When I was a university student, the intellect was a comfortable arena.

That was not always the case.

When I was a young boy, my grandmother used to have to chase me around the fields to bring me back to the shade tree on our farm, where an Ethiopian Orthodox priest used to meet us for a day of study. I had a lot of energy, and I wanted to play and run, but because of the arrangement my father had made with our tutor, I had to sit under that shade tree with my brother, Tafari, and wait for the priest to arrive. When you are a 6-year-old, waiting is torture, and escape is always a temptation. I would try to sneak away, but my grandmother would have none of it. She was determined I should be educated. Imagine what it looked like at that time and compare it to the advantages kids have today.

My grandmother's single-mindedness as far as my studies were concerned had a lot to do with the fact that my own father's education was abruptly interrupted when he was a young boy. He was enrolled at Ballabat School, later named Medhanalem High school, and currently named Gullele High school. The Second Italo-Abyssinian War, the Italian occupation as it is better known, had left its scars on my grandmother – psychically and personally – so whether I liked it or not, this friendly but domineering old lady would track me down and drag me back to that shade tree. When she had me in her clutches, I would surrender. Crossing my grandmother was not a good idea. She was dark-skinned and fierce, an Oromo through and through.

Looking back, I owe much to her perseverance – or maybe I should say – interference. Without her, I do not think I would have become a doctor. In fact, her influence goes beyond my choice of profession. I am certain I would have perished if I weren't so mired in my studies during the political unrest in the capital during the 70s. My medical studies forced me to stay on the periphery of the student protests. Unlike Yohannes, who could ace his university tests even after sleepless and rowdy nights in the cafe, I needed to apply myself whole-heartedly to my books, a "handicap" that probably saved my life.

The night after we gathered in the cafe, Yohannes disappeared from our dormitory. I knew in my gut the outcome was not going to be favorable. Yohannes Wolde Michael was a very good person. He could fill a room with intellect and laughter within five minutes even though he has no charisma– and he also could persuade without offending you. While a gifted person would be prized in most societies, the government in Addis was not receptive to the opposition of any kind. The Dreg didn't trust the student population, and Yohannes was a member of EPRP (Ethiopian People Revolutionary Party), operating a bookstore. Many student leaders were murdered, and others disappeared into the forest to start an armed struggle. Meles Zenawi might have disappeared at that time. I did not know him personally, but my other friends knew him. A few students who completed General Wingate high school made it to medical school. I finished high school in Ambo, Haile Selassie's 1st secondary school. Today I see Ambo as a center of the freedom movement. It is a center where people voice the core issues about Ethiopia. Poet Tsegaye Gebremedhin was born and completed his high school education in Ambo.

Yohannes was from Kambata region, an impoverished area in southern Ethiopia where too many farmers scrape inset (a plant resistant to draught) and coffee from the ground. It is a district that tends to grind not only coffee but its best people. But not Yohannes; despite his impoverished background, he was energetic and inclusive. Fortunately, we had already, or at least the university students among us yielded our ethnic differences inherited from our parents. In the 70s, we decided we were first and foremost Ethiopians. Yohannes reminded us of that simple fact daily. He had enormous potential as a leader, and, as a result, he was a target of the government. Recently I learned that there are so many young and vibrant people who are true heroes!!! Ethiopian heroes. This generation brought back Ethiopia, which I felt when I was young.

No one knew where the cadre that burst into his room in the middle of the night took him, but everyone was convinced he was murdered. We had good cause to think about it. The next day, the bloodied bodies of students appeared all over the streets of Addis Ababa. Hundreds of them. Yohannes's body never showed up, but we felt we had enough circumstantial evidence to surmise that he was dead. Yohannes was strong and courageous, but we knew his chance of escaping from the clutches of so many blood-thirsty soldiers and cadres was nonexistent.

I knew many of the slaughtered students whose bodies were strewn in the streets personally. Another medical student who was involved in the student movement met a similar fate. Most of us felt Emanuel's days were numbered

– he was very vocal – but no one anticipated how it would unfold.

We discovered later that a pharmacy student named Tamiru had prepared cyanide tablets and distributed them to the student leadership. When Emanuel anticipated his capture, he swallowed the tablet of cyanide just before the authorities put their hands on him. He died in the hospital where we had our rounds. His suicide did not appease the authorities. The Cadres circled his immobile body in the hallway, then the Duke of Harar Hospital (Current Black Lion Hospital) kicked and spat at him. They then chanted, "Death to the anti-revolutionaries!" Tamiru attended the first-year college with me at Haramaya college, and then he joined the school of pharmacy. He was an outspoken and very sociable person. I learned that he was captured tortured, and killed by the regime. Tamiru was a close friend of Samsom Legesse, who had attempted to assassinate Mengistu Haile Mariam and was later captured and killed. Tamiru and Samson were very close when we were at Haramaya college. Tamiru was very sociable and talkative, while Samson was quiet and introverted.

Everything held dear began to crumble. The capital was mass confused. People were running through the streets; the sound of gunfire was constant. It was a city under siege. Many were paralyzed with fear, especially since the students who were natural-born leaders had already "disappeared."

No one was prepared for what happened next. An internal dispute within the Dreg (the new Dreg General Aman Andom did not want to eliminate members of the royal family) led to the execution of 60 government officials on November 24, 1974. Gunned down were Lij Tsehafi Tiizaz Aklilou HabteWold; Leoul Ras Asrate Kassa; Lij Indlakatchew Mekonnen; Ras Mesfin Sileshi; Lieutenant Colonel Tamrat Yigezu; Kibur Ato Akalework Habtewold; Dr. Tesfaye Guebre Egzy; Ato Mulatu Debebe; Ato Abebe Reta; Dejazmach Solomon Abraham; Dejazmach Legesse Bezou; Dejazmach Sahlu Difaye; Dejazmach Workneh Wolde Amanuel; Dejazmach Kifle Ergetou; Dejazmach Worku InqoSelassie; Dejazmach Aemero Selassie Abebe; Dejazmach Kebede Ali Wele; Colonel Solomon Kedir; Afe Negus Abedge Debalk; Kibur Ato Nebiye Leul Kifle; Kegnazmach Yilma Aboye; Kibur Ato Tegene Yeytechawork; Kibur Ato Solomon GuebreMariam; Kibur Ato Hailu Teklu; Lij Hailu Desta; Blata Admassu Reta; Fitawrari Dems Alamirew; Fitawrari Amde Aberra; Fitawrari Tadesse InqoSelassie; Lieutenant General Abey Abebe; Lieutenant General Kebede Guebre; Lieutenant General Diresse Dubale; Lieutenant General Abebe Gemeda; Lieutenant General Yilma Shibeshi; Lieutenant General Haile Baykedagne; Lieutenant General Assefa Ayene; Lieutenant General Belete Abebe; Lieutenant General Issaya GuebreSelassie; Lieutenant General Assefa

Demissie; Lieutenant General Debebe Haile Mariam; Major General Seyoum Gedle Ghiorgis; Major General Goshu Kebede; Major General Tafesse Lemma; Vice-Admiral Eskender Desta; Brigadier General Mulugeta WoldeYohannes; Brigadier General Wondimu Abebe; Brigadier General Girma Yohannes; Colonel Yalem Zewd Tessema; Colonel Tassew Modjo; Colonel Yigezu Yimene; Major Berhanu Metcha; Captain Mola Wakene; Captain Demesie Shiferraw; Captain Belay Tsegaye; Captain WoldeYohannes Zergaw; Corporal Tekle Haile; Private Bekele Wolde Ghiorghis; Lieutenant General Aman Mikael Andom; Lieutnant Tesfaye Tekle; Corporal Yohannes Fetoui. It was horrifying. Imagine the chaos if 104 American senators were executed for disagreeing with the President of the United States. That is the situation we were dealing with in Ethiopia in 1974. That marked the start of lawlessness in Ethiopia. This is a nation rich in history and culture. This is the nation that fought colonialism and crushed outside invaders. On November 16, 2020, the electoral college voted and declared Joe Bided the next president of the United States. New York Times editorial published an opinion page that stated The Republican Who Embraced Nihilism and stated that the Supreme Court thwarted the latest Trumpets' attack on American democracy. What happened in 1974 in Ethiopia is shocking, and what happened in America during Trump's leadership has lowered the decency and dignity of human intelligence. How do we explain January 6, 2020, Capitol Hill riot to overturn an election in the US?

A week later, the new government closed the university. They literally shut the doors and began moving the students out of the capital and into provincial towns in the countryside. Before I could even consider returning to my parent's home, I was given the assignment to go to the southwestern part of the country, where thousands of students were herded into camps. The government called it a national campaign for development through cooperation to further land reform – villagization – but the real motive was to disperse the students to get them out of the capital and under more direct surveillance. It was a simple plan: get rid of the leadership, then clamp down on dissidents. The military junta had recently received millions of dollars from the international community for the famine that had claimed the lives of 300,000 people in Tigray and Wollo provinces. Instead of addressing this problem of famine, they used those donations to divert the student population.

I was in my second year at medical school, but the military officers put me in charge of the medical care for nearly 10,000 students. I was overwhelmed. There was medicine – for the students who quickly succumbed to malaria and gastroenteritis – but there was no medical equipment. I felt powerless as conflict erupted almost instantaneously. The military continued to round up students and kill them; the farmers were angry by the influx of students and were fomenting their own uprising; even the students were quickly becoming politically divided. Fighting broke out everywhere – every day – even without overt provocation. So, when I wasn't administering to the students who were becoming ill from the unsanitary conditions in the camp or malaria, I was dressing wounds or removing bullets from shattered legs and arms. It was non-stop crisis management.

I was fortunate. While many students were forced to live in tents and hastily built thatched huts, I resided in a comparative luxury place. I shared a room in a local nursing school along with a few other students, as well as some college professors and administrators.

At first, I just wanted to hunker down and stay put in my room at the school. I think I was in shock. The provincial towns were ruled by violence. And hiding out seemed justifiable since no one really knew what to do. The authorities were not giving us any direction. But isolating in a room can be its own torture, so I ventured out as soon as I could calm my nerves. It took a few days to muster up the stamina and courage.

The camps were a mess. Everyone was sick or fearful. I felt deep anguish, too. My life had suddenly become unanchored, unruly, and unmanageable.

The first few weeks in the camp mirrored the chaos in the capital. The only thing we could be sure of in the provincial town was constant terror. Working under these conditions became nearly impossible. I had to react quickly to crisis after crisis, but too often, time was wasted, and lives were lost. Political discussions about Marxism and Leninism were possession among students.

If I had not been given a job to do, I probably would have folded in the chaos and confusion. Administering to the sick and dying forced me to become single-focused. I woke up each morning with a pain in my gut and chest – absolute dread. To get myself moving, I would pray and take deep breaths. Eventually, I would get dressed and walk to the makeshift clinic to do whatever was necessary. For those first few months, as incomprehensible as it sounds, a medical student oversaw the healthcare for thousands of students.

Obviously, I made my fair share of mistakes. But the situation was so critically out of control that I had to just move on to the next crisis. I did not have time to think about my missteps, which made it seem even more unreal that the authorities continued to look to me for direction. It was not until word spread to the rest of the world about the famine-stricken areas that we started to get outside help in the camps.

I would have preferred to go back to the capital, but I was not allowed, so I showed up to assist doctors at the regional

Nekemte hospital. As we waited for the university to reopen, there was nothing else to do. But I was grateful I was able to put my novice skills to use. I wanted to help. And after I thanked God that I survived those first few months, I also thanked Him for another gift. By the time the camps settled into a semblance of normalcy, I had developed a composure that even the most practiced doctor would have envied. Nothing rattled me.

This composure was probably one of the reasons why I caught the attention of the Swedish surgeon, Dr. Svene Holmberg. On a weekly basis, Holmberg would drive 150 miles to the provincial town, Nekemte, to care for the wounded and perform elective surgeries and then turn around two days later to drive back to Addis Ababa. He was fearless. You had to be fearless to volunteer to drive through the Ethiopian countryside in 1975. The mountains were treacherous, the terrain was unforgivable, the military was unpredictably aggressive, and the rest of the population was conditioned to kill you if you took them by surprise. I greatly admired him for this alone.

I assisted him during his surgeries at Nekemte Hospital, and I had an opportunity to become even closer to him. I was, in fact, awed by this man's inherent talent and selflessness. He had an enormous reserve of energy and creativity, especially under miserable conditions. And I believe he liked me because, after a few months of camp life, I was unflappable and steady. Dr. Grima Melaku, MD, a general practitioner at that time in charge of the hospital, was very supportive to me and offered me tremendous help and guided me. We have become friends since then. Girma is a great physician with solid conviction and integrity.

I worked side by side with these doctors – happy to allow others to be in charge – doctors much more skilled and experienced. Oddly enough, as a result of working with these doctors, my own confidence returned. When I was on my own, I made mistakes. Mistakes that would keep me awake at night and render me less useful the following day. But I soon found out from the other doctors that I had gotten many things right. After a few months of assisting at Nekemte Hospital, the Swedish surgeon proposed that I ask for a release so I could work in one of the Swedish mission hospitals in another province.

I jumped at the idea. While living in the camp had improved from those first few weeks, it was still intensely draining and heart-wrenching months later. Literally and figuratively, I was putting Band-Aids on wounds that needed 100 stitches. I used to fantasize every night that they would reopen the university so I could resume my former life. When Doctor Holberg suggested a way out, my heart lifted. The only problem was that getting a release was not a simple procedure. The authorities were not going to be easily swayed.

I ran a million ideas through my mind about how I was going to garner this release, and then I finally succumbed to the oldest excuse in the book: I told them my mother was ill (while secretly praying that God would watch over her and not punish me for lying). The authorities gave me the release – even though I hadn't seen nor heard from my mother since I was a small boy. I was given a positionat the Swedish mission hospital in Ballesa, Kambta, after about ten months at the camp. The lesson I got from this is to jump on an opportunity when it comes and to fall forward.

It is miraculous when you come through a dark tunnel in your life, and you finally see the light. My new position made me feel like I had been given the keys to eternal happiness. I worked and was paid $50 per month – a fortune under those circumstances – at a small clinic, basically run by two American nurses. Even though I was still hoping that normalcy would return, and the university would reopen, in the meantime, this position was essentially an answer to my prayers – short-lived as it was.

I wish I could say my family fared as well during this political unrest. My father, Asfaw Gamachu, was a successful farmer and district governor under the feudal system. When the authorities confiscated his land in 1975, his life and livelihood were threatened. He battled with the authorities when they came out to his property, a few soldiers were killed, and his aid was also shot dead, and he was forced to go into hiding and on the run. He escaped to the mountains, but his house at Tulumara was burnt to the ground. He witnessed this from a nearby forest hill, and he told me later that he had said to himself, "You burnt my property, but you did not burn me."

This was not our family's first brush with violence. My grandmother had lost more than her son's education during the Italian occupation, where more than a million Ethiopians perished (some from mustard gas approved by Mussolini). During the war, my grandmother's husband was conscripted by Haile Selassie's army to go to the battlefield to join a half million other Ethiopians. My grandfather survived the war but was met with a violent outcome upon his return from fighting the last battle against the Italians at Maychew, a battle that claimed the lives of 10,000 Ethiopians. My grandfather lost at battle his younger brother Kuru Moticha.

Even though Ethiopia has more than 80 nationalities speaking 84 different languages and belonging to almost as many different religious communities, relations between many of these groups was often harmonious. My grandfather befriended comrades from the battlefield and brought them home with him. His intention was to establish a resistance to fight the invading Italian army. The problem was that a united front against the Italians did not necessarily translate to a friendly unification between the Ethiopian tribes. My grandfather was an Oromo, the largest ethnic group. His new friends were members of the Amhara, Mursi, Dizi, and Chaha tribes. There was a dispute about inviting these people into his village, and my grandfather was shot – right in front of my father, who had just turned 18 years old. The story of this event was told nonstop in our when I was a child, and the courage of my father to break his father's gun into pieces so that others do not possess it. He came out victorious by overcoming adversity at that moment.

It is the story that drives and determines a family's future. My father was thrown into the role of a family leader as a result of my grandfather's death by assuming charge of the farm. Whether he was ready or not, he was pressured to make decisions that would not have been had his father died of natural causes. My situation in Addis Ababa in 1974 carried the same overtones. I, too, was plucked out of my own medical apprenticeship and violently thrown into an arena I was not fully prepared to enter. Events like these can ruin you – or make you stronger.

My position at the Swedish mission hospital, under the tutelage of the two American nurses, did not last long. After three months, one of the nurses running the clinic had to return to the United States unexpectedly. The American nurse who remained quickly became overwhelmed and applied for a transfer. Luckily for me, there was a rumor that the university was about to reopen. I hurried back to Addis

Ababa. On my way back, the bus that I was riding in overturned, but I survived, and there were many injuries.

I did not recognize the city. I immediately went to the dean of the medical school and asked him what the plans for reopening were. Confusion and chaos were still the order of the day. Although there were no longer dead bodies strewn in the street, the capital was still barely functioning. There were food shortages, blackouts, unruly crowds, and threatening cadres everywhere. Still, it was better than being stuck out in the provincial towns, where conditions were deplorable and malaria was rampant.

Although I knew there was not much of a chance that the university would reopen soon – given the pandemonium in the capital – I wanted to at least hear about some definite plan to reopen. When the dean suggested it might take another year, he must have read the disappointment on my face. I asked the dean, Professor Demisse Habte, if he could help me find a job to keep me going while I waited to resume my studies. He was sympathetic. The dean put me in touch with his friend, Dr. Craig Wallace, who was the head of the US Naval Medical Research Unit in Addis Ababa.

It was more than I expected.

This was an incredible opportunity. I was sent to the division of biological research and infectious diseases, and my job was to examine samples. While it may not sound like heaven to some, I planted suspensions of ground ticks, mosquitos, and organs taken from birds in two-day-old mice and then isolated the virus. For the most part, I spent most of my day in the lab removing the brains of baby mice while Dr. Owen L. Wood, virologist; my mentor, and supervisor, looked over my shoulder and made quiet suggestions. It was the kind of work that transported me to another plane. I could forget about what was going on in the streets and even in my hometown and focus my concentration on something that would benefit others.

It was intricate work, and it suited my temperament. I felt great joy working at the Institute – for the first time since Yohannes Wolde Michael had been apprehended. I realized then that everything in my life had brought me to this point. While I was unhappy about the state of my country and worried about the fate of my family as well as myself, I also realized good things occur even in the darkest hour. People extended a hand and helped. I just had to be willing to receive that help – not always when I wanted it, but at the time, it was offered. Patience was necessary. I was glad I had developed it – waiting under the shade tree waiting for my teacher to show up.

Chapter 2: Plucked from the Forest

Our neighbor, Aba Tamiru, knocked loudly on our door. That is not his name, but in Ethiopian culture, to respect a person, you call that person the father of X, and in this case, his son is Tamiru. I often saw Aba Tamiru chatting with my father in the fields. I would watch how the two men leaned close in as they spoke to each other – familiar but respectful. The only time I remember Aba Tamiru entering our house was when someone was ill. That day I mentally inventoried everyone in my household: my sister, my brother, my father, my mother, my uncle and his family, and my grandmother. As far as I knew, everyone was well. My mother had been busy all morning cooking, cleaning, and fussing. Her demeanor was different when she was caring for a sick family member. Then I noticed something.

Aba Tamiru, who was tall, lean, and darker in complexion than the forest without a moon, was wearing a shawl and carrying a very sharp knife. My eyes widened. I was four years old. There are nights – to this day – when I can still recall every feature of Aba Tamiru's face.

Both of my parents immediately came to the door and took me by the hand. I was escorted to the living area. We lived on a farm, and the house – a compound that housed my uncle's family as well – as the only one in our village that had a corrugated roof. This distinguished my family. It was built by my grandfather, Gamachu. And, unlike so many others, we had a room where the family gathered. My grandmother came out of the kitchen rubbing her hands on her smock after cooking. Everyone looked calm, but I was puzzled.

It is customary to perform circumcisions in Ethiopia. Nearly every male child in Ethiopia is circumcised. Nowadays, it is done in a medical facility with a nerve block. Back then, it fell upon the shoulders of my neighbor, the village healer, to perform the procedure – with the blade he was carrying and without anesthesia.

When I realized that afternoon that Abu Tamiru was pointing his knife at me, I began to scream. No one else seemed alarmed. They were smiling and consoling. My father held me down. But it was my mother I looked at as I struggled to free myself. I was appalled. Why didn't she help me? I could not believe she just stood there – sympathetic but useless. I was placed on a large table, and the healer took his knife and cut my foreskin. It was excruciating. And bloody. When you are young, this much blood gushing from your own body makes an indelible impression.

My mother tucked me into bed immediately after the circumcision. I think everyone ate a big meal. I cried all day long – and stayed in bed for a week. And it was weeks before I could go out to the forest and gather wild strawberries with my brother and the other children. I had to content myself with fresh milk from my cow. In OROMO tradition, every child has a designated cow. It was the only thing I could keep in my stomach anyhow.

Besides the physical trauma of the circumcision, I felt scarred by the procedure. I read once that circumcision negatively alters the perinatal brain and affects infant-maternal bonding and trust. I often wonder if being circumcised when I was four years old – and the pain I associated with it – had anything to do with my reaction a year later when my mother and sister left the family home. I do not know when the practice of circumcision started in Oromo culture. In the book of Genesis Chapter 17, God ordered Abraham to obey the terms of the covenant. He was ordered, "Each male among you must be circumcised" We learn in this chapter that every male child must be circumcised on the eighth day after his birth. This applies not only to members of your family but also to the servants born in your household and the foreign-born servants whom you have purchased. Ethiopian orthodox church gives equal importance to the Old Testament and the New Testament. Male circumcision is an important part of Islam. Oromos in the area of my birth were more influenced by the Ethiopian orthodox church rather than Islam. However, in Oromo culture, 'Wakafacha' worshiping God is more emphasized. They consider God is universal.

Without any drama in the household, my mother moved to a town named, Shambu, where her brother lived. I was surprised by their departure, but I did not ask any questions. I was close to my father and grandmother, so the loss did not seem acute. I woke up one morning and my mother and sister were gone. My grandmother slipped effortlessly into her role.

Looking back, I can almost understand how my parent's divorce happened. The house in Tulu Mara with the corrugated roof belonged to my grandparents and housed my father's large extended family. My mother was greatly outnumbered. When my grandfather was shot in front of his son (my father), it was my grandmother who managed to hold the pieces together until her three sons gained some maturity. Ethiopians are known to be tall and regal, but my grandmother was a small, strong, and sturdy Oromo – a compact woman with an iron will and deep resilience. When my father married my young mother and brought her back to the farm, my mother must have recognized that she would always be an outsider – an afterthought – in that household. The farm was my grandmother's fiefdom. She had the final word.

I adored my grandmother, but it can be difficult to flourish under such a strong presence indefinitely. Even my father needed some distance. Of course, my father's decision to drift away from the farm and go to Bako was under the guise that he was gaining some power of his own. He became involved in administrative duties at the woreda in Bako, and would travel, sporadically at first, by mule for the entire day to stay in the small village until his business was finished.

The children stayed with their grandmother during this time. By now, my mother had quietly returned my sister to my father's farm. Again, it was mysterious to me. My sister seemed to appear out of nowhere after being gone for a few years. My sister was nine years old when she returned. She looked a little different, but for the most part, she had not changed all that much. I was seven years old, and my brother was six years old, and we honestly did not pay that much attention to our older sister.

I do not think any of us had words for my mother's actions. We just sensed something was wrong between our mother and father. And we could read in our grandmother's face that it was better to leave it be.

The position in Bako grew more demanding, and I suppose appealing, as time passed. My father traveled more frequently and was away for long stretches of time. He eventually had to peasants to help my uncle, Zelke, manage the family's farm. The children went about their daily routines – studying with the priest and wandering through the forest when we had a chance to escape from our studies.

Most people can't imagine allowing their own children or grandchildren to play freely in the wilderness – too many visions of lions, tigers, and bears – but when I was a child in Ethiopia, we spent every opportunity we could steal gathering berries and chasing antelope under the forest's thick, cool umbrella. While it is an entirely different story today, nearly half of Ethiopia was covered with trees 50 years ago. Dense forests covered the topography. In fact, nearly every farm was surrounded by a long-stretching canopy of trees.

Ethiopians used to consider these forests sacred, a place where all God's creatures could abide in equanimity. Adults often romanticize their childhood haunts – whether it was the panoramic vistas of coastal dunes or the blacktop city streets that served as baseball diamonds. I am not unique in that way, but I think I have a good case for saying that the forests in Ethiopia were paradise to a child. Heather and tall grasses fought with Juniper for gnarly space while the antics of colobus monkeys and baboons struggled for a child's attention. Birds who could add a few colors to Crayola's 64 were everywhere. Wild pigs, hartebeest, and shrews made our playtime exciting and adventurous – with just the right touch of threat. My brother and I loved playing in the forest.

Which made my father's decision to move to Bako a year later that much harder for us. Not only would we be leaving our beloved grandmother, but we would be living in the new, small house my father built in the village of Bako – with his new wife, Ejigayehu. My grandmother never betrayed her sadness about the children leaving her. Instead, she continually talked about the schools, the hospital, and the wells – as though these modern advancements more than compensated for any attachments we had to her, the farm, or even the forest. Fetching water from nearby brooks was made possible by her maids, they carried clay pots on their backs. She was proud of my father, telling us that he had been instrumental in the building of new schools. That's all she seemed to talk about the few weeks before our departure.

She prepared our food for our full-day journey by mule to Bako – and she did not shed a tear when she said goodbye.

Bako, in southwestern Ethiopia, was a new experience for us. About 2,000 people resided there when we arrived – and true to my grandmother's claims – it had new schools, a marketplace, and a medical facility. There were rumors that it even had telephones and cars, although when we first arrived in Bako, I never saw any. It would have seemed like Disneyland to us if it had not been for my father's new wife. Ejigayehu who did not like us, and we did not accept her. Although she was strong-willed like my grandmother, she was also hard, scolding, and abrupt.

She was not from our region. In fact, my father had met her in the capital, so her manners were foreign to us. And we could not find any love in her heart to even remotely resemble the affection our grandmother had for us. To make matters worse, my father's administrative responsibilities in the town grew – he had a regional position now – and he began to attend night school. Egijayu had no children of her own, so she resented us. The children decided she was only tolerable when my father was around. Generally, we gave her a wide berth – staying away from the house whenever we could.

The good news was that we were immediately enrolled in the new government-run school that my father had helped build. We are Oromos, the largest tribal population in Ethiopia and democratic by nature. Although only 5 percent of the Oromo population is literate, we value education and see it as an opportunity to break out of the cycle of poverty. My father was dedicated to the eradication of illiteracy – and determined to do something about it, even if it meant getting his own hands dirty. Thomas Edison once said, "Opportunity is missed by most people because it is dressed in overalls and looks like work." When it came to education, my father made sure he did not miss these opportunities. He got out his overalls when it was necessary.

The recently built primary school was bright and airy – with a flagpole in the yard near its own soccer field – and boys, as well as girls, used to gather there every morning to sing the national anthem. Director Alemayehu was enthusiastic and hopeful – and, as a result, so were we.

Ethiopia was embarking on a new future – and we felt as though our generation was going to be part of it.

For the first time, my brother and I did not have to rely on our cousins or the shepherd's children for companionship. At our new school, we were not limited in the number of friends we could make. In fact, we had so many school chums that we had little time to think about our grandmother, Tulumara, the forests, or our own mother. We immersed ourselves instead in our soccer games and our studies: history, geography, mathematics, and gardening. Haile Michael, who was a police officer at Bako, was a very close family member, and his mother was my grand father's sister. He was a cheerful and loving person and replaced my father whenever he was absent.

Gardening was an important part of the curriculum at schools in Ethiopia, which is understandable since it is a nation regularly devastated by famine. When I was young, the government blamed the famine on the farmers. Their cultivation methods were outdated, and they degraded the land with deforestation, or so the government claimed. In turn, the farmers accused the government, saying the only thing the officials cared only about was the cash crops, such as coffee and sesame, that they exported. The truth is that famine in Ethiopia can be attributed to many factors – with drought usually being cited as the main culprit – so water is a consuming passion in Ethiopia. Ethiopia is blessed with numerous rivers.

We had no water at our new school, so we had to carry it from our homes to cultivate the gardens we grew. While we did not have running water in our home, we did have wells in the yard – one of the modern conveniences my grandmother rhapsodized about when she told us about Bako. I planted a fig tree to celebrate one of the many graduation ceremonies we held each year at the school. Every day during my third year of schooling, I was required to haul water to the schoolyard from our family well to soak the baby tree. I was amazed when I went back for my father's burial in Bako after several decades; the little fig tree had managed to survive and grow despite the calamitous drought that decimated nearly 300,000 Ethiopians in a famine in the 1970s. Recently, on July 30, 2019, Ethiopians embarked on a reforestation program and planted more than 353 million trees in a day under PM Abiy Ahmed's leadership. He continued to lead in watering the plants.

Like the early Californians, Ethiopians treasure water. In fact, I don't think it is any coincidence that mythically it was water that lured the Queen of Sheba into King Solomon's bed. In many respects, Ethiopia's royal dynasty owes much to a glass of water.

But beyond our royal dynasty, many anthropologists consider Ethiopia the birthplace of humanity. Chair of the

Norwegian Nobel Committee, Berit Reiss- Anderson, stated that we are all Ethiopians on the 11th of December 2019 at the ceremony held to award Nobel Peace Prize for 2019 to PM Abiy Ahmed. And we are also distinguished in modern times. Ethiopia and Liberia were the only two African nations to resist European colonization, even during the "Scramble for Africa" years. The country remained steadfastly independent – and fierce. Haile Selassie may have claimed to be a direct descendant of the Queen of Sheba, but so did every other Ethiopian leader before him.

We are a proud people.

My father, comparatively speaking, prospered in Bako. We were one of the few families to own a car. When I was ten years old, I might have perished if it were not for the family's VW Beetle that raced me to a neighboring hospital when I was delirious with malaria. I recovered in Makemte Hospital, where I was given chloroquine. I recuperated in a day or two, which is not unusual when proper treatment is administered quickly, but my recovery still seemed miraculous to both my family and me. I was given a "wonder drug," chloroquine. This experience stirred my initial interest in medicine. I was out of my mind with a fever – on the verge of dying, my family said – and yet I recovered. I was lucky. Malaria kills more than a million people a year in the subtropics. Being spared made a deep impression on me, and medical breakthroughs were very much a part of my personal story. But besides medicine, my near-death experience also stirred something else in me. * picture of VW and me

To this day, I have an affinity for the VW Beetle. But my love affair with cars started earlier when I saw my first movie the year before malaria. Terefe Negero, chief of school health services in the capital, hooked up the school projector to a car engine, and on a regular basis, we would gather to watch health-related movies at the school. Despite everything that was preoccupying the grownups of Bako during the late 50s and 60s, no one could convince the children watching those movies that the world was not full of promise and wonder. That same year in Baku, an Italian man, Vitale, a leftover from the Italian Occupation of the 1940s, figured out a way to generate electricity from a diesel engine. For the first time, our town was awash in light. We could now read in the glow of a lamp at night. New worlds were opening. You can see how backward Ethiopia is. I was in third grade when our home was suddenly crowded with visitors from Addis Ababa. They were Tigist's brothers and cousins and their families. It was a scape from the confusion in the city due to an attempted coup by General Mengistu Neway, who was the commander of the Imperial bodyguard Unit. Emperor Haile Sellasie had left of an official visit to Brazil. The coup was set to start on December 12, 1960. Many government officials were assassinated, and there was fighting in the city. The plan failed in a few days, and the emperor interrupted his visit and landed in Asmara, and the situation normalized. Our visitors also went back to their homes in Addis.

I believe that young Ethiopians can learn something from the past and travel back to their realm of thinking. In February 2022, Ethiopians celebrated the generation of electricity from the hydroelectric plant at the Grand Ethiopian Renaissance Dam, which caused a lot of political turmoil from Cairo to Washington, DC. The Arab league, the Sudan, middle East nations, and the European Union all were involved. The colonial-era agreement was violated by Ethiopia, and this is considered a new Adwa by all Ethiopians!

Chapter 3: Crossing Hao Janjero's River

My father at his farm in Tibe

Our household grew. My father was well-respected in his home village of Tulu Mara. His father had fought against the Italians, our family sustained itself comfortably on our own farm, we were involved in local Oromo politics, and we valued education and advancement, so it was really no surprise when one of my father's many godsons from Tulu Mara arrived in Bako and moved in with us. My family was going to help further his education, and I was ecstatic. It meant having another friend close by – under our own roof, in fact.

Unlike Americans, Ethiopians do not normally prescribe to the nuclear family. We are tribal by nature, so it is not unusual to see large clans of people living under the same roof peacefully and fruitfully. My father was comfortable with this arrangement – it seemed natural to him – but not to his wife.

Although we never openly complained to our father about Egijayu's behavior, I think he sensed our fear of her – at a time when his administrative duties were taking him farther and farther away from home. Even though we avoided Egijayu whenever possible, her tirades became louder and more frequent. My father got the picture. They eventually separated while we were in Bako – and we were all greatly relieved.

For the most part, Ethiopian children do not concern themselves with the affairs of adults. In the Horn of Africa, there was too much competition for our attention. When we weren't involved in the activities at school – soccer, gardening, studies – we explored the surrounding forests, mountains, and the Gibe River. The wilds of Africa were our back yards, our playground. The boys in our family loved to fish, and we would escape to the river every chance we got.

The Gibe River is a muddy tributary of the Omo River. It separates the Shewa, wollega, and Kafa Provinces, but it is not too wide or deep to wade across, even for a young boy. Gebre, my father's godson, and I decided to excuse ourselves from our Saturday chores and venture out to the river to do some serious fishing. We escaped from our home unnoticed and entered the forest stealthily, looking for wood to shape our rods. It took us an hour of scouring the forest floor for the perfect pole. Somehow, we knew instinctively what these poles should look like, and we were not satisfied until we came upon two perfectly straight branches to attach our string. We used onion for our bait. We were now ready to snare our catch.

We waded into the river and immediately cast our rods. The water was only up to our thighs, so we ventured out farther – just past the middle of the river – and had not come to a full stop when Gebre's rod was jerked out of his hands violently. We both jumped for the stick and pulled it back into our grasp. I let go once I realized that Gebre had a firm grip on the pole and resumed casting my pole while I watched my companion fight and tug with his prey. I felt a pang of envy that my line remained inert through the whole spectacle.

Gebre Yohannes was a year older than me. Even though I had many advantages he didn't have, I looked up to him. He was a year older than my ten years, and that one year seemed to be the difference between wisdom and ignorance. I was thin and agile, but Gebre was taller and sturdier, showing the first signs of his own virility. I could hold my own on the soccer field with him, but not in the water that day.

The commotion stirred up in the muddy waters by the tug of war between Gebre and his catch was ferocious. Gebre tugged and tugged. I could see the muscles in his arms bulging with effort and strength. I was in terrible awe of him as he struggled with the unknown aquatic enemy. I could not take my eyes off him.

Finally, Gebre shifted his weight and fell back into the water. Suddenly a snake doubled the length of the two of us put together and sprung into the air. We screamed in terror. It looked more venomous than Hao Janjero, the mythical snake god of the Gibe that alternately disguises itself as a crocodile one minute and a snake the next. In our worst nightmares, Hao Janjero looked benign compared to the snake Gebre had gripping onto the end of his hook. We screamed, and Gebre threw the rod into the river. We scrambled with every ounce of adrenalin to the other side of the river.

When we fell onto the shoreline, I began to laugh hard because I felt as though I was on the verge of crying. Gebre had his face in the mud of the shoreline. I thought he must be laughing, too, because he did not raise his head up from the mud for a few minutes and his shoulders heaved as he caught his breath. I realized when he looked up that he had succumbed to what I managed to hold at bay – gut-wrenching fear. His face was caked with tears. I felt a small satisfaction wash over me, the kind of feeling you get when you have just withstood a test and come out ahead of the person who intimidated you. I laughed deeply – but not from fear this time – and Gebre finally began to smile and laugh.

The sun was going down, and I knew that sooner or later, we would have to re-enter the river to cross to the other side to get home. I certainly was in no mood to confront that demon swimming around in the Gibe River with a hook in its mouth and an onion in its gullet, but I knew we didn't have a choice. Our home was on the other side.

Gebre stubbornly refused to budge. He said he would never go into that river again – no matter what. I looked at the horizon and considered our options. If we didn't leave soon, we would have more to worry about than the snake. The river was full of crocodiles, and the shores could get unfriendly after dark as well. I pleaded to Gebre to get up and let us make a run for it to the other side. He refused.

I looked at the setting sun again. I had to resort to another form of coaxing by scaring the wits out of him by telling him what our chances were of surviving the night if we didn't cross the river and get home immediately.

The look of cheer and relief that he felt once he knew we had escaped from the demon in the river drained from his face. He may have been dark as night, but at that moment, he was as pale as I had ever seen him. His dread was evident, and he argued vehemently that he would not go back into that water. I resorted to more stories of humans being eaten alive by nocturnal predators.

He finally relented, but Gabre insisted we walk down the river and cross in a place that seemed worlds away from our destination – and that venomous snake. I appeased him and walked. We would be late in coming home, but I also preferred the possibility of my father's reprimand to the chances of meeting that viper again. And I was secretly pleased when we dashed through the water to the other side, and Gaber beat me to the shore by a length. I joked about his pure unadulterated fear for weeks. His age advantage suddenly disappeared.

My father did not wait long before he brought another woman into his life to take Egijayu's place. Her name was Tigist Bezu (Amharic word that means patience in abundance). The children immediately fell in love with her because she was full of good humor, smiles, and affection. Even though she had no children of her own, the whole tenor of the house changed with Tigist in charge. Laughter filled the rooms of our house in Bako, even when new family members showed up and came to live with us. Tigist was tolerant and embracing of all the children, and I remember it as a happy and peaceful time for our family. I didn't want it to ever end.

Professionally my father's influence was growing. He had expanded his reach considerably and was now raising money and removing obstacles in the building of a school for Tulu Mara. Although the government supported the extension of educational reform throughout the country, many areas in Ethiopia – where there was a dire need for primary schools – were inaccessible. Roads needed to be built so building materials could be brought in, and hurdles with local officials had to be surmounted. Fortunately for Tulu Mara, when it came to education, my father was indefatigable. He threw every ounce of effort into the project, and the school was eventually built.

His commitment to education had a profound impact on his children. We mingled with the teachers and administrators at the school, books were brought into our house, and our admiration for schooling continued to grow. My father was required to take frequent trips to Addis Abba, the capital, and whenever I could accompany him and spend my time in the marketplace picking up used books, which I would bring home with me and read. My tastes were not refined. I read everything I could get my hands on.

Although I would have been content to remain within the confines of Bako forever, the world was growing larger. Not only was I reading about distant lands and foreign cultures, but I was venturing out more and more as I approached adolescence. I was accompanying my father on his trips to Addis Abba more frequently. You would have thought I had traveled halfway across the continent whenever I visited the capital. It seemed like an entirely different world, and I was beginning to recognize that Bako had its limitations, but I had no desire to pick up and leave. My horizons were large enough.

But then our father came home one day and announced that we were moving – leaving Bako. I was devastated. He had been assigned to a government post in Gedo, about 50 kilometers from Bako, and I would be starting the 6th grade in a new school, and I would have to make new friends all over again. The only good news about this cold and foggy region was that we moved into a house twice the size of the one in Bako – and, predictably, so did many of our relatives.

The house was full of children within a year – my uncle's children, friends of the family, cousins, and Godchildren. I was rising up in the ranks – at least in terms of my age. The only one older than me was my sister, but she was two years behind me in school because she had missed out educationally when she disappeared with my mother for those few years before we went to Bako. There were many mouths to feed in Gedo, and I'm sure my father was not concerned about that.

On one of our trips to the capital, I bought a book on raising chickens. Since there was nothing you could not learn from a book, I decided that I was ready to put the book's words into action. With my trusty book and guidance from one of the agriculture teachers at my school, I bought my first chicken. I cared for it solely – without any help – and got it into my head that it might be a good idea to expand and buy a few more chickens. I sold a few of my books and bought some more chickens. This went on until I was able to grow my coop to more than 100 chickens.

I became the family entrepreneur, and those chickens gave me a new status in the family and in town. I could buy things for myself that I never had access to before. I could help provide breakfast to my brothers and sisters – a very empowering feeling for a child. I enjoyed the feeling immensely, so much so that I would become visibly annoyed with my father and Tigist every time they confiscated one of my chickens to use as a gift for another family.

Unlike Bako, life in Gedo was not all fun and games. I was growing up, and my responsibilities in the family grew as more children from our extended family came under our roof. At one point, there were 12 children living in our house in Gedo. Before we all traipsed off, though, I would assign the younger children's chores. They helped me in the chicken coop, and those who performed their chores to my satisfaction were given an extra egg at breakfast.

I did not care for the school in Gedo, but I did continue to play soccer vigorously and managed to find my place in the new school eventually. By the time I was in the 8th grade, our team was so accomplished that we won the championship in our region, and we had to travel to Ambo to compete in another championship game. We won the game!

At about this time, when I was at the height of my soccer fervor, a peculiar event occurred in my family. My older sister was pulled out of school. She was still behind me in classes, even though she was 16 years old. At first, I imagined it was because her academic prospects seemed limited, but then I found out that my father was beginning to make arrangements for her marriage.

The women in Ethiopia are different from the women elsewhere. They are stoic to the core, and difficult to read their emotions. They have a level of acceptance that is so deep that it makes them veritably unfathomable. My sister did not complain or betray any disappointment when she was removed from her classes and told that she would be given away in marriage.

Back then, no one in Ethiopia considered these arranged marriages a violation of human rights – as they do today. To this day, in rural Ethiopia, nearly half of the girls are married before the age of 15. Back then, in some respects, my sister was considered old. Her "bride price" – the amount a groom's family pays to the bride's family – was quickly dwindling. This did not actually impact our family, though, because my sister's arranged marriage had little to do with poverty and everything to do with power.

It would increase our status because Beliyou was marrying into an esteemed family in a neighboring region. For most of that year, my father and Tigist decided for a huge wedding – full of pomp and ceremony. My sister acquiesced and made no indication that she was displeased. She accepted this fate – of leaving her family and going to a new one – as did so many other women in Ethiopia at that time. The wedding took place when she turned 17 years old. When she left her home, she was accompanied by her maid so that she felt at home there. It signaled more changes to come for my family.

The wedding was not the only disruption to our family structure. The town of Gedo did not have a high school, and my father was determined that I continue my education. I would have to leave and go to another town. When I graduated from primary school, I sold my books and chickens and headed to Ambo.

It was a culture shock for me. Ambo was ranked as a First-Class Township, and its educational system was considered one of the best in the country. When I enrolled in my new high school, I was surprised to discover that Haile Selassie Secondary School was so much more competitive than what I was used to in Bako and Gedo. Academics had always come easily to me, and for the first time in my life, I had to work hard in the classroom.

Nearly 50,000 people live in Ambo at that time. I had never lived in such a congested area. I lived with a family who were close to my parents. Colonel Tadesse Mekuria and my father were close friends. Tatek, col Tadesse's son, is my father's godson. So this family is considered my family. To make matters more competitive, the school system absorbs students from neighboring woredas, mostly Oromo, and the atmosphere can become highly charged with this thick concentration of bright students.

I had become something of a kingpin back in Gedo – sure of my place in my family, school and soccer team. In Ambo, I often felt out of my element and unanchored. It was lonely and difficult at first. I missed Tigist, the children, and especially my father. I did not feel at home until I joined the Boy Scouts, an organization that helped bring me back to my initial interests in nature, swimming, and community involvement.

Nestled between Mount Wenchi with its crater lake and the Guder and Huluka Fall and elevated 6,800 feet, Ambo is considered a spa resort – more beautiful than Gedo or Bako. There was telephone service, a grand hotel, medical clinics, a post office, and an array of restaurants. But it was the natural landscape, as always, that intrigued me.

Ambo is also world-renowned for its thermo-mineral springs. I suppose with all that water around; it became apparent that it was time I learned to swim. Under the tutelage of the scoutmaster, I immersed myself in a new sport. I became a swimmer. If the mineral springs of Ambo were good enough for the royal family and other Ethiopian dignitaries, I figured I might as well try it myself. I loved it. I felt as though there were now no boundaries I couldn't cross – mountains, lakes, rivers, forests. I was 17, and I felt like I was finally beginning to know my way around.

Family get together at Gedo, my grandmothers seated.

Chapter 4: Choosing Doubt over Dogma

With my classmates at Ambo High School.

Ambo and the capital had a symbiotic relationship. There was a constant spilling over of ideas, culture, trends, students, and unrest. Most experts claim this has more to do with the student population than proximity. Ambo is 125 km from Addis, but the educational systems of both cities are comparable. Serious students, in other words, are drawn to both densely populated locales. Some even consider the Ambo schools to be superior. And that initially posed a problem for me. This is what I wrote about my childhood at Ambo. Now I live in New York, and the years I spent there made me what I am today.

As I mentioned, I was surprised once I got to Ambo that I had to struggle in my classes. I was always an avid reader, so my coursework came easily to me in Bako and Gedo. Not so in Ambo. At Haile Selassie I Secondary School, built in 1943, there were two tracks of education – one track for university-bound students and the other track for vocational students. If I didn't work harder than I was used to working, I knew I was going to miss out on the classes for college-bound students.

I poured myself into my books. The sciences were my initial attraction, but I had to branch out and read and study whatever I could get my hands on. Math and English had to be mastered. Fortunately, the teachers, many of whom were Peace Corp volunteers or foreign-born Indians, were helpful and willing to go out of their way for students who showed an interest in their studies. In fact, in 10th grade, I had a teacher from India who offered me private tutoring in mathematics – free of charge. I went to his house several times a week for a few months. I would not have done well without him.

I met many young men in Ambo whom I admired: Tesfaye Hundessa, who was first in our class, and Zebib Gayem, who was second. Both were fun-loving fellows who took their soccer as seriously as they took their coursework. I admired them and wanted to consider myself their equal – at least academically. I became very motivated.

Although my first year in Ambo was difficult, things settled down by 10th grade because my parents moved from Gedo to Ambo, and I no longer had to live with my uncle's family sharing a bedroom with my cousins. I could set up my own schedule and get the support I needed at home to further my studies. Tigist Bezou, my stepmother, who I had grown to love, was encouraging. In fact, it was Tigist who suggested I consider a medical career. She said I "had the nature for it."

I don't know exactly why she directed me this way, except that there had been a family friend – whose illness affected me deeply. Our friend was a strapping man with a big laugh and a strong build and personality. Everyone loved him, but when he developed heart failure, his legs and belly swelled with edema making him almost unrecognizable. Suddenly the man who could fix anything and mesmerize any crowd was reduced to a bloated shadow. He died at what should have been the pinnacle of his life. He was 45.

I was old enough to understand what death meant – and I was devastated. After he died, there were many discussions in our household about the importance of getting medical care – and I was often chosen as an example because of my bout with malaria – so I somehow felt personally tied to this man's fate.

Tigist noticed my bewilderment over our friend's death – the endless questions – and made a mental note of it.

Although my father never pressured me one way or the other as far as my studies went, there was a prevailing attitude in my household that, eventually, I would take charge of the family farm. Agriculture was, after all, in my blood. Still, Tigist encouraged me to explore the sciences – she pointed me in the direction of books when she couldn't answer some new perplexity. And I was more than happy to comply. When I couldn't find what I was looking for at home, I went to the school library. I developed a reading habit.

Darwinism was a passionate topic of study at my school, probably because while I was in high school Richard Leakey and his team had discovered fossils, which were considered the earliest fossils of Homo sapiens in sites near Kibish in the Omo River – the very same waters shared by the Gibe River where the snake god nearly had us for dinner. Ethiopia was now considered by the entire world the "cradle of Homo Sapiens." In fact, the fossils of Omo 1, found in 1967, directly resemble the bone structure of modern man. To an impressionable young man, the evolutionary history of 195,000 years in your own backyard can stir up all kinds of thoughts in active imagination.

I believe it was these lively class discussions about evolution that sent me searching for other answers. By the time I reached the 11th grade, I wanted to reconcile my religious beliefs with my academic pursuits. I had stopped pestering Tigist for answers and had now turned to my friends instead. During the winter break, which is the rainy season, the high school closes for a few months. During that long lull, my friend Zebib, who could not answer my incessant questions about the meaning of life and the origins of man, suggested I enroll in a Bible study class at the American Baptist Missionary nearby.

Since the rainy season always limited our options on the playing fields at school, I decided it wasn't such a bad idea.

I studied Christianity with the same vengeance at the American Baptist Mission that I attacked my studies at Haile Selassie Secondary School. I was fierce. By the time I had matriculated to the 11th grade, I was ranked first in my class, and I brought this determination to Protestant Christianity – and tackled every book of the Bible, from Genesis to Revelations – at a time when Omo 1 was taking up equal space in my brain.

I was swimming in contradictory thoughts and ideas, but I relished the stimulation – even though, at times, it was downright confusing. I was so immersed in the Bible for those few months during the rainy season that I considered converting if our winter break didn't come to an end, who knows what would have happened! But the rain did come to an end, and I decided I better apply myself to studying for the Ethiopian School Leaving Certificate, which I needed to pass if I wanted to go on to college.

I set up a study group that included my close friends and was surprised that Zebib did not plan to join us to study for the test. My friend, a Jehovah's Witness who initially encouraged me to study the Bible at the American Mission, was convinced that a college education would be pointless ... when the world was about to come to an end. Zebib was an excellent student, so I was perplexed when he was unable to hold all the contradictions of the universe without hurting his own chances at a future. His beliefs were a personal disadvantage and caused him harm. That was my conclusion, so I became leery of dogma. Although I enjoyed every moment of my Bible study and felt gratified to be able to talk about God in a new way, I decided that my Ethiopian Orthodox faith was sufficient – and not that much different from Christianity in many respects – and I did not convert.

It was not my first disturbing brush with dogma, though. While I was in the 11th Grade, I entered an essay competition sponsored by the Peace Corps. The winner of the competition would secure a spot as an exchange student – in America, no less. I spent many nights reworking that essay repeatedly – an essay about why I wanted to become a medical doctor – and I won the contest. The excitement about going to the States as a student nearly turned me into an insomniac. I was ecstatic.

Then it happened. The American Ambassador attended a fashion show at the university in Addis Ababa. Students in the capital had been grumbling about his visit, so there was tight security, but the fashion show got out of hand. A disturbance ensued, and the Ambassador was pelted with rotten eggs by the students. In the aftermath, the exchange program offered by the Peace Corps was cancelled for the year. I lost my chance to go to the United States of America. All because of eggs.

I could not think of another person I knew in those days who loved the world of ideas more than I did, but suddenly, in 11th grade, I was beginning to grow skeptical. It was the second time in a year that an idea was taken to its illogical conclusion – doing more harm than good in the end. I was sorely disappointed by my friend, Zebib, a Jehovah's Witness. And I was sorely disappointed about that rotten egg incident, which prevented me from following a dream to discover the world.

I think I would have been in sorry shape after this experience in 11th grade if it weren't for the other friends I made at Haile Selassie I high school, some of whom I am still in touch with today. I was especially close to Nega Seyoum, a bright young man studying arts and humanities at the high school. We shared many interests. Nega's father was from Eritrea, and he had fought the Italians for five years during the Occupation. We looked alike too. Many people, in fact, mistakenly identified Nega as me. The teachers were confused; my own relatives were confused … we looked so much alike. In many respects, I know what it's like to have a twin, which can be convenient when you have an overdue book at the library, or you spurn a young woman's advances. You're safe … at least temporarily.

Fortunately, in 12th grade, Nega Syoum and I passed our entrance exams for college. But unlike Nega, I decided to attend Haramaya College of Agriculture instead of going to university in Addis Ababa. I wanted to make sure I was making the right decision as far as my family and medicine were concerned. Although I would just be taking general courses at Haramaya in the first year, I needed to know that I was more suited for medicine than agriculture. I have a deep love for the country, and I thought that this passion for the landscape might interfere with my interest in healing and the human body.

In retrospect, Haramaya was the right choice. Life was quiet and conducive to studying, which was not the case in Addis Ababa. Many of my friends, in fact, did not make it through their first year of study at the university in Addis Ababa. Besides the heightened student unrest, there were too many competing distractions in the city. In Haramaya (then called Alemaya), I did not have a choice but to study. The campus is tucked away in the mountains, about 500 km from Addis Ababa, and it overlooks Lake HaraMaya and Gara Mulata Peak. Half of the land is cultivated, and the other half is filled with meadows filled with modern buildings, flowers, trees, and pastures. It's a beautiful spot – and at times, I felt tempted to forsake medicine and instead go back to the land.

In my first year at Haramaya, I became friends with a professor, an American named Wendell, who shared my love of nature. We often took trips in his Fiat out to the countryside to make use of our new cameras. We would photograph everything, and I have happy memories of stumbling upon some of the most awe-inspiring landscapes. It is easy to understand why the mountains and forests in Ethiopia were often considered sacred.

Much to our dismay, the student unrest in Addis Ababa began spilling over into other university towns, and I was deeply offended when a group of Marxist students at Haramaya accused Wendell of being a CIA agent. It was laughable to me, knowing Wendell, but I think the English professor was deeply wounded by their taunts. He encouraged me to read African series of books published by famous authors such as Chinua Achebe. Yet all this suspicion on the part of students gave me an uneasy feeling. You tended to start questioning yourself – looking to see if you have blind spots.

This incident also reminded me that there was no escaping the escalating unrest. I had to decide about my future – medicine or agriculture – and after studying for one year in a country where even an innocent can be accused of the most ridiculous accusations, I decided to apply for a premed school in Addis Ababa. Along with 28 other students, I was accepted. I packed my bags.

But before I could say farewell to Haramaya, I had the opportunity to attend the graduation ceremony of final-grade students. It was quite an event. Haile Selassie I, our Ethiopian leader for the last 50 years, would be attending. I was thrilled when I was seated two rows from this international celebrity. Although Haile Selassie was taking the heat elsewhere – being blamed for the escalating violence on the borders of Somalia, the poor working conditions in the city, and even the famine – he was still a legend in Africa.

He was even a legend in the world. In 1936, Time Magazine had crowned him "Man of the Year." And, 35 years later, to his credit, Haile Selassie had managed to keep Ethiopia at the forefront of African independence and progress. He was also deeply committed to education, which won him favor in my education-thirsty family. I was glad I had stayed for the graduation ceremony – until one of my good friends came up behind me and whispered in my ear that they had just arrested a man who was impersonating me in the dormitory.

It turns out that while I was attending the ceremony, a thief broke into my dormitory room and walked out with one of my best woolen suits on his back. That day I had another twin – this time, one not as friendly as Nega. My friends got a good laugh that day. In all the commotion, I missed Haile Selassie's speech, but I did get my suit back. And I must admit it made a sad departure from the beautiful Haramaya Agricultural College campus a little easier. At the very least, I figured that the incident at the very least would prepare me for the city life ahead in Addis Ababa.

Of course, in 1973, the threat of thievery was the least of my problems in Addis Ababa. The city was a cauldron of disturbance. At first, I didn't pay much attention to it all. As usual, my coursework and professors at the Institute of Medical Sciences were the focus of my attention. I was apolitical. Not because I distrusted the government or found the topic boring but simply because I had other interests. Namely, medicine.

The medical school in Addis Ababa was the only one in Ethiopia at that time, and it attracted some of the best – and most idiosyncratic – teachers. Our pharmacology teacher, Professor Howarth, caused a stir because he believed that concentrating on areas of science before there was a basic understanding of medicine was a waste of time. In many respects, his holistic approach was ahead of its time, but he did not gain any fans from the faculty. They took potshots at him incessantly – saying he was stepping on people's feet by teaching subjects that were the terrain of other professors. He was a huge favorite of the students because he was so unconventional – learning from him was fun. Barber Raily, who was a physiology professor, created unnecessary stress with his antics – putting his chair on top of the table and making the students jump from one microscope to the other in rotation to answer quizzes on what they saw. Howarth got a lot of pressure from the academic community for his integrated approach to learning, and eventually, he resigned but not without causing quite a stir in the student body. We started to question the administration's policies.

Not to say that it was difficult to stir us up. It was the early '70s, and like other students worldwide, we were beginning to believe we had a voice in what went on in our colleges as well as our countries. We were sometimes impatient with the dean of the medical school, Sir Ian Hill, who was the former personal physician of Queen Elizabeth. Even Getachew Bolodia, the only Ethiopian professor on staff, should have inspired us with his erudition but instead irritated us with his pomposity. We rolled our eyes every time he reminded us that he studied with Crick and Watson, the fathers of DNA and former Nobel Laureates. Authority no longer carried the same weight.

The world was changing, and I was getting a new view right there in Addis Ababa. Our lens was finally going beyond the parochial – making us, for the first time in our history, just as concerned about the Apollo space landing and the assassinations of Robert Kennedy and Martin Luther King as we were about our aging emperor. Students in those days zeroed in on what was happening to us on a grand scale. For someone who had a long history of reverence for education, I was surrounded now by students who questioned everything. That kind of environment eventually rubs off on you. I, too, began to look at the status quo in a different light.

In 1973 Martha Sibhatu, a senior medical student, and Wallelign Mekonen, a radical student leader, were killed in the air while attempting to hijack an Ethiopian Airline. That was a sad moment because the student movement converted into an act of terrorism.

But I was glad I discovered in my formative years the hazards of dogma. As a university student in Addis Ababa, I decided to remain open-minded but detached – making sure I could embrace justice without turning around and rigorously denying other people with opposing views their own rights. I made up my mind – as a future doctor – that if I could not heal, at the very least, I would do no harm.

Chapter 5: A Rift so Deep

With my nursing staff at St Mary hospital, Axum.

A recent study in Geophysical Research Letters reported that Ethiopia has an ocean in its future. Atalay Ayele, a professor at Addis Ababa University, and a team of other scientists from around the world explained that a 35-mile rift in the Afar desert in Northern Ethiopia shows a crack, which measures 20 feet wide at intervals. They claim the rift is analogous to the early formation of an ocean (replicating oceans already in existence). While the Ethiopian ocean won't develop any time soon, these scientists predict that the Red Sea will eventually flow into Ethiopia's new ocean.

It was the thought of this veritable sea change that caught my attention. I didn't think there could be a greater rift in Ethiopia than the one I experienced while I was a university student in Addis Ababa. My world had turned upside down – and I couldn't imagine it ever being so disruptive (even during the Italian occupation) with all the different factions vying for power all at the same time. Chaos, confusion, death, and destruction were the prevailing forces in Ethiopia in the early 70s. I fell out of love with my country.

Haile Selassie had been emperor since 1931, and his health was failing in the early 1970s. He had modernized Ethiopia while maintaining independence – and had even drawn up a constitution and resisted imperialism by insisting all enterprises were at least partially owned by Ethiopians – but his power was ebbing. He is considered the father of the African Union because he was the founding father.

A devastating famine in the Wollo province had killed approximately 50,000 people – and there were accusations that Haile Selassie and his government tried to cover up the extent of the starvation. People were outraged. To further alienate the royal family's following, there was an oil shortage. While Americans had to wait in long lines for gas on alternating days in 1973, Haile Selassie imposed a 50 percent tax on petroleum – without allowing the cab and bus drivers to adjust their own prices. The transportation system was severely debilitated as a result, and the drivers went on strike. The economy was on the brink of collapse.

To deteriorate the general mood of the country even greater, the fight for independence in Eritrea had exhausted resources, and the military now threatened to challenge the government over a pay increase and living conditions. Haile Selassie's cabinet resigned. Teachers threatened to strike over poor pay and limited educational opportunities. Farmers were grumbling about land reform. And the students responded to all this unrest by asking for a change of government – hoping that a new government would align with the burgeoning Marxist and Socialist ideology that was sprouting up among the country's urban intelligentsia.

Most historians and political analysts believe it was Haile Selassie's failing health that brought the country to the tipping point. Our emperor, after all, had not prepared for a smooth and strong transfer of power. But, more realistically, it was a combination of several factors – all coming together at a time when enormous rifts were occurring inside and outside the country. The key was that Haile Selassie faltered and left an opening for the second most powerful opposition – the military – at a time when the country (and the world) was vulnerable.

A military commission of about 14 officers was formed in response to this opening. These were men who had risen through the ranks as opposed to an elite force that was part of the emperor's Imperial Bodyguard or appointed by the crown council. While the ragtag military commission still claimed allegiance to Haile Selassie, behind the scenes, they were vilifying the emperor and destabilizing the new cabinet. Rumors of corruption and the opulence of palace life – even a documentary featuring the emperor's pampered dogs – were showcased in grim relief to the starving in the north of Ethiopia. The people, especially the students, started to turn against a once-popular monarch.

On September 12, 1974, a small group of officers – headed by Major Mengistu – went to the palace and demanded Selassie's resignation. Colonel Debela Dinssa read the statement that requests the resignation of the emperor. In full military regalia – proud and unflinching – the emperor signed off and was put under house arrest by the commission. He was driven out of his palace in a beetle volks wagon. Volks wagon was my favorite car because it saved my life when I got sick from malaria at age seven in Bako. My parents rushed me to Nekemte hospital in volks wagon. The Derg, Amharic for "committee," was now in control of Ethiopia.

Soon after Selassie was forced to resign, the "bloodless coup" turned ugly. On November 23, 1974, "Bloody

Saturday" as it is now known, 60 men – generals, cabinet officers, one of Haile Selassie's grandsons, and various other members of the royal family – were executed without a trial. The media announced that Selassie died from respiratory failure during a routine prostate operation on August 27, 1975. His doctor, Asrat Woldeyes, claimed there were no complications. As a result, speculation that Selassie was assassinated persists to this day. It sent an alarming chill throughout the country – as well as through our family. Tigist's brother, Legesse Bezou, a member of the cabinet, was one of those executed. My mother was terrified.

And my father was deeply worried, too. On December 20, 1974, the Derg issued a Declaration of Socialism, announcing that businesses must be publicly owned, and agriculture collectivized. Military officials tried to arrest my father while he was at his farm in Tulu Mara, but he resisted and went on the run. I was disturbed by the news, but again I felt helpless.

At that time, medical students in their first year were moving their rotations from Princess Tsehai Memorial Hospital (named after H. Selassie's daughter who had been a nurse in Great Britain while he was in exile during the Italian occupation) to a new hospital called Duke of Harar Memorial Hospital (later named Black Lion Hospital). We were excited by the opportunity to work in an environment that was technologically superior to the old hospital and perform groundbreaking services. The medical school was now in a new modern building. Switzerland doctors were running the hospital, and they gave superb services.

We also had an opportunity to have a short rotation at Addis Ababa Fistula Hospital, the only hospital of its type in the nation. Because many women in Ethiopia undergo genital mutilation and are pregnant at a very early age, they suffer from complications during childbirth and are predisposed to fistulas. Fistulas are debilitating and create incontinence – fecal as well as urinary – which renders many of these women outcasts in their own villages. The Hamlin's, obstetricians from Australia, developed a surgical treatment to address this medical issue and opened a midwifery school and hospital to cater to these women. The story of the Hamlin's and Fistula hospital is fascinating.

Medically speaking, we had a right to feel excited about our future. There was no doubt that our country had made significant progress, despite all the political commotion and turmoil. The medical students at the university hailed from Cameroon, Zimbabwe, Kenya, and, for the most part, they were enthusiastic and brilliant – and thoroughly committed to improving medical services in Africa. Although the possibility that we would be sent to war fronts in Somalia and Eritrea upon graduation loomed large, we also felt as though we were in exactly the right spot to make real and significant changes in our country – at least medically.

I say medically because most of the medical students did not participate in the political upheaval and student unrest in the capital. We were too focused on our studies – which were intense – and it was understood by the rest of the student population that medical students, at the very least, had other things to worry about besides Marx and Lenin, namely, things like malaria, relapsing fever, fistulas, smallpox, starvation, and innumerable other diseases. I wish the military had shared this view.

When the Derg decided to shut down the university, many of the foreign medical students left the country. We lost good future physicians – doctors like Abraham Varghese – to medical schools outside the country. To compound matters, our administrators, the head of the surgical unit, and the dean of the school had to refocus their efforts on fighting to keep the school open as opposed to curing disease and improving medical care. Asrat Woldeyes, professor of surgery and dean of the medical school at that time, fought single-handedly against the interruption of medical education in the country. He never backed down, even though his anti-communist views put him at odds with the Derg regime. When he officially spoke out about the death of Selassie (he was the emperor's personal physician), his views got him into further trouble. The Derg wanted to get rid of him. He was temporarily reassigned to Massawa, where he treated the injured – from both sides – of the

Eritrean War. Dr. Ambachew Woreta worked at the war front with him.

The closing of the university was devastating. I probably wouldn't have survived if it weren't for the intervention of innumerable family friends, and strangers.

Life was difficult when the students were dispersed to the countryside. To make matters worse, it wasn't just about our own hardships. Most of us were deeply concerned for our families. My father was in hiding – and there were times I didn't know if he was dead or alive – unless I reached out to my brother, which carried its own dangerous complications. My brother kept in contact with my father, but we had to be careful about openly communicating about his whereabouts during the Derg military regime. Too much was at stake. My father was on the run, and frequent communication was counterproductive to his safety.

I tried to remain objective and detached during this period. I attended to my duties – administering to the students' medical needs out in the countryside – while the capital underwent a bloody siege of power. The worst was hearing about friends who had disappeared or been murdered. That's when it was most difficult to remain objective. But we were also scared – terrified, in fact – that at any moment, we could find ourselves looking down the barrel of a gun and having to explain our beliefs or even our existence.

It is times like these that you must go inside to your inner reserve – to summon up every ounce of honor, dignity, and courage. I was surrounded by young men and women in the countryside. We were all doing the same thing – questioning ourselves and our predicament – rather than enjoying ourselves in the cafes and study halls of our youth. Thousands of young people gathered – or dispersed, I should say – and there was, amid the chaos and disruption, an internal quiet that still amazes me. That was mindfulness!!

To this day, I count my blessings that I did not stay longer than a year out in the country with the rest of the students in the provincial town, that people intervened, and I was given employment while I waited for the university to reopen. Dr. Sven Holberg, a Swedish surgeon who visited Nekemte hospital every two weeks to perform surgery, got me temporary employment in a rural missionary hospital in Bellessa, Kambata. When I returned to Addis, Doctor Demissie Habte referred me to Dr. Craig Wallace, who was instrumental in helping me work in a research laboratory that he oversaw, American Naval Medical Research Unit (NAMRU3) in Addis Ababa. I will be indebted for the rest of my life for the help I received from these men during a dangerous time in my life. Each of them went out of their way to help me. And knowing these men, I am sure that I was not the only one who benefitted from their kindness.

While Addis Ababa was in chaos and dead bodies were appearing on the streets out of nowhere, I was fortunate that I was injecting mice with the grounded specimen of mosquitoes and ticks and organs from birds collected by a field team and trying to discover if new viruses were on the verge of infecting the Ethiopian population and nation. Diseases do not respect national boundaries. I learned so much in this research laboratory – techniques and procedures that I would employ in my later career as a doctor – that my mind was full of hope for the future rather than despair for the present. Dr. Owen L. Wood, my mentor, and supervisor in the virology laboratory, changed the route I would take in medicine and steered me away from negative thoughts. The work kept my mind occupied while my father was on the run and my university studies were interrupted.

After about two years on the run, my father eventually negotiated with the military and surrendered. He was alive, and that was a relief, but he was subsequently arrested and put into prison – a man who had spent a good deal of his life raising money for roads and schools and bridges and hospitals. It didn't make any sense, but that is usually the case when aggressive men are jockeying for power and destroying anyone or anything that impedes their path.

Ethiopia had always had an understanding with the United States – Haile Selassie made sure of it – but now, with the Derg in power, Mengistu's brutality, the EPRP, and

MEISON radicalism and the Russians and Cubans moving into the city and the countryside, the relationship became strained. The American Mission was closed, and many Americans were expelled from the country. Naval Medical research Unit was closed.

I eventually left my research assistant job because the medical school was reopened. There were shortages of everything in the city. It was tense. There was a 9 p.m. curfew every day, and different factions were fighting and creating havoc. The medical school reopened amid this disruption. We were expected to pick up where we left off, which was impossible unless we developed tunnel vision.

I did not commit myself to any ideology, but Socialism was on the tongues of my fellow students. I was curious. I was also angry with the situation, so I explored the concepts and talked about the alternatives to the situation we all found ourselves in. I did not embrace Socialism, but I was young, so I was intrigued by new ideas. When I wasn't studying my medical books, I was reading. Many of my close friends began to refer to me as Bertrand Russel because I read everything by the philosopher and writer Bertrand Russell.

We resumed our clinical rotations, despite what was happening in the capital. There was a new crew of doctors: Russians and Cubans, so we had to reinvent ourselves and adjust our thinking so that it aligned with the new status quo. We did a lot of pretending during those years – everyone did.

And most of the medical students – all Ethiopians now that the foreign students had left the country – buried their heads in their books. We worked very hard to graduate … and to keep our sanity.

As soon as I started my internship at Black Lion hospital, I decided to visit my father, who was in prison at Ambo, my old high school town. I got off a minibus and headed to a hotel where I could spend the night before seeing my father the next day.

I never made it to the hotel. Instead, I was approached by a cadre and escorted to the police station, where I was locked up without question. The next day, I discovered that my father was in the adjacent room with another group of political prisoners. I joined them in the morning, but I could not explain to my father why I was there. While I was hoping to cheer my father with my visit, I could see that my imprisonment aggrieved him terribly – so much for my good intentions.

Surprisingly, although the jail was small and we had to sleep on the floor, I did not find it unbearable. My experience in the provincial town with all the students had obviously hardened me so that I could withstand quite a bit of discomfort. And ultimately, I was happy to see my father. He was thinner but not emaciated. He looked old, but I embraced him right away, and we spoke for hours – about the family, my studies, my future, and about my father's future. Once my family heard the news of my imprisonment, they paid regular visits and began to visit us at the jail – bringing food and other provisions – and expressing outrage that the authorities had locked me up. They contacted all the local officials to protest this new turn of events.

I was surprised by the kindness of the guards. They did not treat us as though we were deviants and thieves. Instead, they acknowledged our situation – and tried to make matters as palatable as possible. After a week of family and friends petitioning, I was released while my father remained in jail.

I had no idea what would become of my father, but I was encouraged that the dynamics in the prison were not as corrupt or vile as what I had witnessed in the capital. I had to keep telling myself that my father was going to survive this experience. He was my father, and regardless of what we had both experienced during the troubles, I still considered my father stronger than me. Perhaps it's a father-son thing. Maybe a son never thinks of himself as more indestructible than the father, but I also think it may have had something to do with the lingering doubt I harbored while in jail.

Although I tried not to let my father see it, I must confess I was worried that my medical studies were going to be derailed yet again, and I began to wonder if God truly wanted me to be a doctor.

I hated leaving my father behind. It was an awful feeling – I suppose it was akin to survivor guilt – but my father insisted he was going to be all right and that I should leave before everyone changed their minds ... that something good should come out of all this mess. I complied.

My father wanted me to complete my internship and become a doctor. He told me that I had gotten this far and that I should not give up right before the finish. All those years on the soccer field paid off. I wanted to beat the Derg. I agreed to leave. I was going to succeed – even though the obstacles kept growing and growing. I was given a sealed letter by the political cadre who put me in prison to hand over to his superior in Addis, captain Daniel, whose office was in the current parliament building. Daniel was amazed at what happened to me and encouraged me, and advised me to go my business without fear.

That's the way it often is in life. The closer you get to your heart's passion, the harder it becomes to fulfill it. I was encountering one obstacle after another, and it was beginning to wear me down. I was discouraged. I was frightened. I was tired. And ultimately, I was sad. The losses were piling up. My father had lost his farm at Tulu Mara; he was in jail; my friends were being murdered; my schooling was interrupted; my mother was afraid for her life; my country was torn to shreds. Ad infinitum. It was going to be one of those tests in life – making a sacrifice for the greater good, even though I felt like folding. I left my father and prison behind and recognized that it wasn't my father who had aged but me.

With friends at my residence in Axum; Left to right Dr. Mesfin Minas, myself in the middle with Alem's daughter, Letebirhan, Alem Teklu.

Chapter 6: 'Blood that Freezes, Blood that Burns'

Graduation was anticlimactic. No one cared very much about festivities, so there were no ceremonies. Everyone had more important things to think about; namely, survival. While I was happy to be leaving Addis, the capital Menelik, emperor of Ethiopia from 1189 to 1916, had created, I was also concerned about my next destination. The news was not good.

Once I completed my medical studies and internship at Black Lion Hospital, I was immediately assigned to work at St. Mary's Hospital in Aksum, located in the northern province of Tigray. Under normal conditions – without the country being torn apart by internal strife, political unrest, and wars on two fronts – being assigned to Aksum would have been a plum assignment. Aksum is a beautiful old city.

This city, a mile above sea level, is the former capital of Ethiopia and sits near the Blue Nile basin and the Afar depression (the future ocean!). Architecturally, spiritually and culturally, the city is significant. Aksum dates to 1000 B.C. and was established during the reign of Queen Sheba. Because of its early gold and salt trade with Egypt, India, and Arabia, the city has retained a cosmopolitan flavor with Jewish, Muslim, and Christine influences blending. Aksum, considering itself an equal trading partner with Egypt, Rome, and India, was the first African nation to issue its own coins in the 6th century. The city even developed its own alphabet: Ge'ez. While not as influential as it used to be, the city is still a bustling center for trade.

But, more importantly, it is also the center of the Orthodox Tewahedo Christian faith and is still considered the spiritual center of Ethiopia, with pilgrims making yearly visits. According to the Orthodox Ethiopian Church, the Ark of the Covenant – the sacred gold-plated container that held the Ten Commandments, Aaron's rod, and the miraculous manna that kept the Israelites alive while they wandered the desert for 40 years – is housed in Aksum and kept under constant watch in a treasury near the Church of Our Lady Mary of Zion. Ethiopians believe that Menelik I, the son of Queen Sheba and King Solomon, brought the Ark back to Ethiopia for safekeeping. Some biblical authorities argue the veracity of this claim, but Orthodox Ethiopians are convinced: The Ark resides in Aksum.

As a new doctor, I would have preferred debating and exploring the authenticity of the most important biblical artifact in the world, but this was not where my energies were pointed. While I should have been spiritually and intellectually stimulated by my stay in Aksum, I was instead focused on the many horrible rumors I had heard, namely that it was an epicenter of guerrilla activity and widespread violence.

When the Derg unleashed the Red Terror against political dissidents in 1977, radical student activists fled to Mount Asimba in northern Ethiopia, just outskirt of Adigrat. Asimba became home to the Ethiopian People's Revolutionary Party (EPRP), a group fighting against the Derg as well as against rival anti-government groups. All this political and student unrest spilled over into the city of Aksum, as did the war being fought in Eritrea.

Once I began getting used to the idea of my new assignment, the reality of the situation sank in. Rumors were soon verified, and I did not like what I was hearing: I was going to be replacing a doctor who had been captured for being a "collaborator." Dr. Abebaw was tortured by Derg cadres for his supposed revolutionary ties. In fact, more doctor-torture stories began to surface as I considered what my prospects were going to be in Aksum. I packed my bags with a dread that I had not known before. I lived in a country where no one had the right to question their "assignments," but this one seemed to be pushing my patience and fortitude to the limit. I felt like I was walking into a trap rather than beginning a promising career as a doctor.

The stories about Aksum continued to plague me. Another doctor, Makonnen Abebe from Adwa Hospital, was also tortured and imprisoned. Dr. Naynesh Kamani was taken by rebel forces from the neighboring town, Adigrat hospital, but at least he was safely sent back. I started losing sleep at night, but I could not figure out a way to bypass the assignment. Those two doctors are currently in the U.S. and have become successful physicians in different specialties.

Regardless of what I thought, arrangements were being made for my departure. I was told I would be met by Solomon Tesfa-mariam, the provincial medical officer, midway, but first, I had to travel by bus north through the mountains. It took most of the day to get to Mekele by bus. I did not know what to expect when I arrived, but I was happy to be greeted by Solomon, who oversaw all the health services for the entire province. He was accommodating, friendly and lighthearted, even though I knew he performed his duties under enormous pressure and stress. I shouldn't have been, but I was surprised to see he was not alone. A driver sat behind the wheel of Solomon's Land Rover, and an armed military officer was in the back seat. I tried not to reveal my discomfort – the discomfort I felt whenever a gun was within 10 feet of my body – but it was nearly impossible. Solomon also carried a gun and pretended to be a revolutionary. My observation about the town of Mekele at that time is vivid in my mind until today. It was a small dust-rugged town with houses built along both sides of a single road running one or two miles. By comparison, Ambo was far more attractive and cosmopolitan, with nice modern hotels and buildings.

Solomon told me about what my duties would be once I got to Aksum. I was shocked to find out that – just out of medical school – I was going to be put in charge of a medical facility because more experienced doctors had been captured and/or imprisoned by the Derg or one of the other guerrilla groups. Doctors throughout the province were targets, regardless of what their political sympathies were … or were not. My inexperience in running a hospital reminded me of my student days when I was transplanted to the countryside and put in charge of the medical needs of all those displaced students. As I was contemplating this coincidence, a man jumped out into the middle of the road. It was dark, around 9 p.m., and the driver would have run him over the man. I would have been more frightened, but the man looked like an ordinary farmer – not a revolutionary.

Immediately the military officer jumped out of the back seat of the Land Rover, flailing his gun. Luckily it was just a momentary standoff, and no shots were fired by either party. The farmer was reassured that we were just "medical people," and the Land Rover was allowed to move ahead unimpeded for the rest of the trip. It was obvious that the rebels had put the farmer up to it, but it bothered me that this poor man could have been blown to bits. And it certainly bothered me that I could have been blown to bits, too. It didn't make any sense.

We were supposed to meet a convoy in Adigrat that night, but by the time we arrived, the convoy had already left. Nothing seemed to go smoothly on this journey full of obstacles. We had to spend a day in Adigrat before we could proceed to Aksum. That overnight stay gave me a taste for what to expect in Aksum.

Adigrat was home to Agazi Comprehensive High School, the only high school east of Adwa and north of Mek'ele, and the town's Catholic junior high school. These two schools were student centers that fomented anti-government dissent. I shared some history with this town since many Ethiopians had traveled through Adigrat on their way home from the last battle of the Italian Occupation in Adwa. I felt like I could feel the agitation in Adigrat deep in my gut – maybe this agitation was historical but more likely, it had more to do with the military base located just outside of Adigrat that added fuel to the already tense environment. I couldn't wait to leave town.

When I finally arrived at St. Mary's Hospital the following evening, the administrators were there to greet me. Not one single doctor was in attendance. I was on my own again. I could use the experience I had as a student out in the provincial town, but this tour of duty would require quite a few more skills. St. Mary's was a small hospital – about 120 beds – but I was going to have to oversee the entire operation – from the clinic to the surgical theater. To compound matters, we were in the middle of a war zone, so I would be treating soldiers from the Eritrean front, military officers injured in guerrilla warfare, and the common, everyday illnesses and calamities that normally befall patients at a community hospital.

At times I felt desperate to speak with a colleague, someone who could provide a little direction and even support. Although I personally knew a doctor in the hospital in Adwa, we could not meet and discuss our situations because both of us were literally held hostage in the town where we worked. You could not go anywhere without a military escort – for fear of being kidnapped or attacked. When I tell my son about my experience in Aksum, he finds it hard to conceive how little choice we all had back during the Derg Regime. The lack of freedom was debilitating. We basically followed strict orders – or we were shot or imprisoned.

I eventually fell into a routine of supervising the clinic and attending to surgery – and doing whatever else was required to keep a small hospital running – and, as always, my work provided solace in a way nothing else could. But I often felt as though I was way over my head in Aksum. It was not until a wounded soldier was rushed into the hospital that I gained some confidence in my abilities and skills.

I was in the emergency ward when a soldier arrived in a military carrier with a bullet in his belly. He had already traveled 20 miles from the front, so by the time he arrived at the hospital, he was very bloody. Luckily the soldier was semi-conscious. Still, I knew how dangerous this type of stomach injury could be, so I decided to suture the wound immediately. First, though, I had to locate the nurse anesthesiologist. I could not leave the soldier, so I asked the head nurse, a very beautiful and competent woman, to find the nurse anesthesiologist, Johannes, so he could scrub in. I tried to keep the soldier engaged so he wouldn't slip into unconsciousness.

The head nurse and the anesthesiologist seemed to appear out of nowhere in minutes. I was greatly relieved to see them and relieved that once I opened the soldier's abdomen, I discovered there was no perforation to the intestine. Just a lot of blood. My hands shook, and my nerves were rattled, but the soldier recuperated. I began to feel as though I could handle the mettle-testing crises that seemed to rock the hospital daily. Later, young Ethiopian surgeons were assigned to a few months' rotations. Drs Girma Melaku and Mesfin Minas made enormous contributions to caring for surgical patients during their rotations.

The Derg, a communist military junta backed wholeheartedly by the Soviets, had pushed the country into Civil War with its tactics. Thousands were arrested and executed without trial during the Red Terror. To make matters worse, fighting broke out all over Ethiopia. The

Somali troops were attacking one front over the Ogaden territory, and the Eritreans were fighting on another front. I could not handle the enormous need for medical care on my own, so two Russian doctors, a husband, and his gynecologist wife, were sent to oversee St. Mary's. Much to my relief, I was able to move away from surgery and resume medical care for the civilians in Aksum.

It took a little getting used to, but I had to refer to Nicholas, the Russian doctor assigned on a permanent basis to St. Mary's, as "Comrade Doctor." These were the small battles I decided not to fight. If "Comrade" was now protocol, so be it. There were more pressing matters to attend to, and I must admit it was pleasant to have some colleagues finally to share the travails of the day with. I thoroughly enjoyed the company of Nicholas and his talented wife. I did not feel so all alone; they provided me with a sounding board – and many hearty laughs. He enjoyed the vodka that he brought with him, and when that was finished, he discovered home-brewed local liquor that is called areke. Communication was difficult because he hardly understood English, and I do not speak Russian.

It can be very destabilizing to be attacked from all sides. I was constantly looking over my shoulder, out the window, and down the corridor for pending trouble. The hospital was under constant threat. The Derg was forced to assign retired soldiers to the dangerous task of keeping watch over the perimeters of the medical complex. Most of these soldiers were war-worn. They had recently retired and were hoping for some peace after a lifetime of battle. They had had their fill of guerrillas – and the military.

Their presence should have given us a sense of security, but the sight of guns always had the opposite effect on me. I could not forget – for a minute – what the daily circumstances of our existence were. Day in and day out, I would exchange pleasantries with these retired soldiers. Day in and day out, I would think about who these men had already killed and who they were about to kill. I tried to distract myself. For about three months, the beautiful head nurse was a pleasant fantasy, as was my friendship with the Russian doctors.

Later one-afternoon, fighting broke out on the hospital grounds. Johannes came running down the hall and grabbed me. He said the rebels were killing the soldiers – the retired soldiers guarding the hospital outside were outnumbered 3 to 1. Johannes hustled me into the X-ray room- a dark room- and told me to stay put. He then went out and gathered a few more hospital workers. The head nurse was not one of them.

We huddled in that X-ray room while gunshots and screams rang through the hospital. Every time we thought it might be safe to emerge from our barricaded room, another shot would ring out. We stayed the night in the X-ray room, learning a little bit more about each other – our hopes, our dreams, our fears, our loves, our families, and our futures.

When we emerged from hiding, we were appalled by the number of dead bodies. The retired soldiers outside were strewn in the most horrifying positions on the lawn. While most of the patients must have fled during the struggle – or at least those well enough to move – some patients lay in their beds dead from bullet wounds or severely injured. The head nurse disguised herself as a patient and escaped the attack. All the medicine had been confiscated, as was all the equipment in the emergency room. We literally had no supplies to handle the emergency we were confronted with. From the operating room, I gazed at all the dead soldiers outside.

I knew these men personally, and I had listened to them talk about their children and grandchildren. I broke down – unable to control my emotions. I kept thinking about all the orphaned children. I had to leave the operating room, so I could cry without a witness. I knew I would not be able to function without getting this deep emotion out of me. It felt as though my hands would never be steady again. I said a prayer for Captain Sultan, the retired Army officer born in Eritrea, who was the head of the unit, who, before the atrocity, I shared a daily cup of coffee with. My survival and escape from this situation is a miracle. This is not the only one, but I have to be grateful to God.

Before I returned to the operating room, I cautiously began to look in the less conspicuous rooms of the hospital for my Russian friends. They were nowhere to be found, so I gave up. I had no choice because there were too many injured in need of my care. Still, it bothered me that I was handling this crisis without their assistance. I prayed I would not find the Russian doctors dead outside. I knew that would send me over the edge.

For two days, the remaining crew at the hospital worked furiously, attending to the wounds of the injured and transporting the soldiers – and even the injured guerrillas – to the airport where they could be airlifted to better facilities in the capital. Since the Russian doctors were nowhere to be found, I was alone – all the efforts and restoring a semblance of order back to the hospital. I later learned that the regional administrator in Aksum named, Yemane Birhan, worked underground for the rebel groups. Did Meles Zenawi participate in that operation? Nobody knows, but they say he is a coward when it comes to moving to a battlefront.

Amid the chaos, I fell deeply in love with the beautiful head nurse, Letebirhan. The staff called her "Gual Keren" because she was originally from Keren, Eritrea. We held on tight to each other. The atmosphere in Aksum at that time was so bizarre that I didn't even hesitate about falling in love with a woman who was married. Lete was not officially divorced, but we already had been so hurt by the circumstances of our disorderly and violent lives that a small inconvenience. She has not heard from her husband, who was assigned to the southern part of the country, for more than two years. She was upset about that. Like so many others in Aksum, we were willing to take risks – but in the name of love instead of hate.

We moved in together and set up a house in a villa on the hospital compound. I had never had such a serious relationship. I was deeply enamored with her beauty, her competence, her strength, and her desire. We both worked tirelessly to put the hospital back together again – so we shared a common cause – and this general sense of accomplishment further enhanced our relationship. Our love deepened.

In the meantime, I had made inquiries about my Russian comrades. Rumor had it that they had been captured by the guerrillas (they were released four months later unharmed). At least they were alive. These were the bright moments I held on to while in Aksum. I allowed the people who were close to me in this city of woe – Johannes, Gebre, Lete – to keep the flame of my life strong and hopeful. I would have perished without their companionship and support. My time in Aksum reminded me of Robert Browning's poem, Love Among the Ruins:

Where the quiet-coloured end of evening smiles,
Miles and miles
On the solitary pastures where our sheep
Half-asleep
Tinkle homeward thro' the twilight, stray or stop
As they crop--
Was the site once of a city great and gay,
(So they say)
Of our country's very capital, its prince
Ages since
Held his court in, gathered councils, wielding far
Peace or war.

Now the country does not even boast a tree,
As you see,
To distinguish slopes of verdure, certain rills
From the hills
Intersect and give a name to, (else they run
Into one)
Where the domed and daring palace shot its spires
Up like fires
O'er the hundred-gated circuit of a wall
Bounding all
Made of marble, men might march on nor be prest
Twelve abreast.

And such plenty and perfection, see, of grass
Never was!
Such a carpet as, this summer-time, o'er-spreads
And embeds
Every vestige of the city, guessed alone,
Stock or stone--
Where a multitude of men breathed joy and woe

Long ago;
Lust of glory pricked their hearts up, dread of shame
Struck them tame;
And that glory and that shame alike, the gold
Bought and sold.

Now--the single little turret that remains
On the plains,
By the caper over rooted, by the gourd
Overscored,
While the patching houseleek's head of blossom winks
Through the chinks--
Marks the basement whence a tower in ancient time
Sprang sublime,
And a burning ring, all round, the chariots traced
As they raced,
And the monarch and his minions and his dames
Viewed the games.

And I know, while thus the quiet-coloured eve
Smiles to leave
To their folding, all our many-tinkling fleece
In such peace,
And the slopes and rills in undistinguished grey
Melt away--
That a girl with eager eyes and yellow hair
Waits me there
In the turret whence the charioteers caught soul
For the goal,
When the king looked, where she looks now, breathless, dumb
Till I come.

But he looked upon the city, every side,
Far and wide,
All the mountains topped with temples, all the glades',
Colonnades,
All the causeys, bridges, aqueducts, --and then
All the men!
When I do come, she will speak not, she will stand,
Either hand
On my shoulder, give her eyes the first embrace.
Of my face,
Ere we rush, ere we extinguish sight and speech.
Each on each.

In one year, they sent a million fighters forth.
South and North,
And they built their gods a brazen pillar high.
As the sky
Yet reserved a thousand chariots in full force--
Gold, of course.
O heart! oh blood that freezes, blood that burns!
Earth's returns
For whole centuries of folly, noise and sin!
Shut them in,
With their triumphs and their glories and the rest!
Love is best.

Chapter 7: Asking Until I Got the Answer

As a doctor, I have often wondered how much pain individuals must go through before they are willing to change their lives. I wonder about this because I found myself in a similar dilemma when I was younger. I ran every option through my mind a hundred times; I considered every pro and con till my head hurt. I delayed; I procrastinated; I denied. And when it was all too much to bear, I did something else.

I am older now, so I am certain that every time I experience unhappiness, eventually, I am going to ask myself what I need to do to change the situation or myself. But when I was young, I did not necessarily seek the solution within myself. Instead, I looked outward for an answer to a perplexing problem. I was in deep psychic and emotional pain in Aksum. I felt trapped and punished.

And my life in Aksum gave me plenty of fodder. I could blame the widespread violence for the deep fear that would seep out of my pores late at night as I lay in bed. I could blame the Derg for creating widespread violence in the nation. I could blame the guerrillas for making me feel so insecure that I rarely left the compound of the hospital to venture out into the exquisite city. I could blame so many external circumstances of my Aksum hospital life for the decisions I eventually made that I am sure I could soak these extreme situations for the rest of my life and still feel as though I was victimized by being born in the wrong place and at the wrong time. Believe me; I could make a case for this when I was feeling sorry for myself.

But when I look back on my life in Aksum, what I really feel is amazement rather than resentment. I feel blessed to have survived such dire circumstances. As a population, doctors, like the policemen who keep watch over neighborhoods like the South Bronx, are immune to the vagaries and vices of humanity. It's difficult to shock a doctor, but whenever I spoke to my colleagues about Aksum, I could see the shock and alarm in their expressions – and sometimes relief that they had escaped such a fate. Aksum was a cauldron of hate, fear, and daily eruptions of violence.

And yet Aksum was also the place I fell in love. To this day, I enjoy recalling the unfettered happiness I experienced the first few months Letebirhan (Gual Keren) and I were living in the villa in Aksum. To be loved by a woman so deeply was really the only liberation I needed at that time. I knew that no matter how harrowing my day had been at the hospital that Lete would understand. She was so attuned at comforting me that all the misery of the world could not have penetrated my heart as deeply as her caresses did. She was an excellent nurse – and that professional capability carried over to our relationship. Born in Keren, Eritrea, her friends called her Gual Keren – the beauty from Keren.

I felt her love, and I think I reciprocated her love, which made the following decision more perplexing. I decided to leave Aksum as soon as I could get a transfer letter and return to the capital of Addis. I look back now, and I often wonder why I was so determined to leave because in spite of how horrific the city was in 1980, I was truly in love with Lete.

This decision broke her heart. She wanted desperately to marry me, even though her husband was not officially an ex. I thought she was an exquisite human being, but, on some level, I was uncomfortable with our arrangement. I held back because there was no denying that there was another man in her life. Because I desired her so much, I did not know how to express my discomfort about her marital status to her. I regret my inability to communicate my confusion. If I had my wits about me, I would have made a better case for myself. As it stood then, though, I made excuses. I said I needed to move away from being a director of a hospital so I could focus on other things – research being my main interest.

The Ministry of Health granted me a transfer back to Addis four months after the hospital was attacked by rebels. I was satisfied that I had restored the hospital to working order. That was my true accomplishment in Aksum. While I did work hard to restore many individuals and soldiers back to health, mending St. Mary's hospital was really my major priority – and subsequent victory. I sometimes think that if love had been my main concern at that time, my life would be very different now.

Even though I was eager to leave Aksum, I was sad getting on the plane to Addis. Lete and I weathered a particularly stormy period in our lives together. She was so confident in our love. She was such a beautiful and civilized woman. It was hard to leave, but I took a big piece of her with me. I carried her in my heart for months – and secretly, I carried her in my heart for years. I often felt like turning around and going back to Aksum – to marry her – but something kept me from doing that.

That something was my profession. I was invited to the Russian Embassy guest house several months after my return to Addis, where I ran into the Russian doctors who had been kidnapped for four months by rebel forces from Axum. Nicholas greeted me with great warmth. He and his wife were safe in Addis. I could never figure out why he did it, but Nicholas had grown a big, bushy beard. They were lucky. I knew so many others who did not escape.

I had a good reputation in Addis as a result of my work at St. Mary's. I was assigned as a medical director of a hospital serving a military training center a few miles away from Addis. Taking the position at Tatek, the training camp meant that I would never reunite with Lete. There was no hope for the relationship now. I pretended to be grateful for the offer, but the thought of staying in this position for any length of time irritated me.

Major General Afework Wolde-michael must have sensed what I have gone through in Axum and assigned me a car with a military plate on it to be used by the medical director almost immediately – quite a luxury in Addis at that time. As much as I love automobiles, the car did not help.

I had become very practiced at not revealing my true thoughts or emotions. It was a self-protective defense that I needed in order to keep myself from ending up in jail or dying even. I was convinced that the only way I would survive what was going on in my country was by developing a false self. It felt as though I had no choice. It was a matter of survival. I was a healer by temperament and choice. It was hard to find my place in this war-torn, violent country of mine. I didn't stop trying, though.

That's one of the reasons I always gravitated toward the university. There was an openness and diversity, and freedom within the university's walls that I could find in no other locale in Ethiopia. I wanted to move away from the military training center and steer myself closer to the university. I was hoping that, eventually, I would train to become a pediatrician, and it looked as though I was finally going to get the opportunity to specialize.

Post-graduate training at Addis Ababa University began, and they were recruiting doctors. In fact, the Chairman of Internal Medicine, Dr. Edemariam Tsega, had recommended that I apply to the program. Everyone in my family laughed when I told them I was going to apply … simply because I had always made it clear that I planned to be a pediatrician. It was a well-known fact that I had a way with children, eggs or no eggs. Even the Professor of Pediatrics at Addis Ababa University, Demise Habte, was perplexed by my decision to go into internal medicine because he thought I would join his department.

What they didn't know was that I secretly admired the doctor who had suggested that I apply in the first place. Dr. Ede Mariam Tsega was an extremely courageous man, and I was influenced by him. He was a pioneer. A true freedom fighter. And I will always be grateful that he was able to establish a post-graduate program in medicine in Ethiopia – an incredible feat under those circumstances.

I gave up the car and the position and Tatek hospital and decided to join a specialization program in Internal Medicine for three years. It is a new program in the country. I found that I was indeed meant to do this. I was going to become, as they said, "Doctor's Doctor."

Doctors of internal medicine focus on adult medicine and have training dedicated to the prevention and nonsurgical treatment of adult diseases. It is odd how things happen. I loved children, yet most of my postgraduate training was dedicated to learning how to prevent, diagnose and treat diseases that affect adults. The more I studied, the more I wanted to study. I became fascinated with my research in infectious disease, and I enjoyed my collaboration with Dr. Eyasu H. Gaber, who, to this day is close to me. Professor Bayou Teklu, who was my mentor then and now lives in Oregon after retirement, is also in contact with me. Both of them communicated to me their life experiences and the establishment of medical education and services in Ethiopia.

When I finally got over my first love, Lete, I became involved with another beautiful lady named Aida Dibaba. I am not bragging when I say she was beautiful. It is not difficult to come across beautiful women in Ethiopia. There are many. Ethiopia has more than its fair share of them. Aida Dibaba's father was a retired air force colonel during Haile Selassie's reign. We kept each other company for months, and it felt like my life was returning to normal again. When she wanted me to meet her parents and family, though, I could not commit myself because I felt as though marriage would interfere with my desire to go abroad. The retired colonel was sympathetic, but her mother, Georgette, was disappointed. And Aida certainly could not understand my decision. In those days, I was living inside my head instead of my heart.

When I was finished with my training, I decided to become further involved in research. I had become youthfully ambitious; I wanted to find a cure – for one of the myriad diseases that regularly devastate Ethiopia – that was my burning desire. I was fortunate enough to get a position at the National Institutes of Health and then proceeded to travel all throughout Ethiopia. I traveled everywhere, collecting specimens, following up with research, and then moving to another town or province. The peripatetic nature of my research suited me well. I never stayed in any place too long – and that was a great relief. The political atmosphere in Ethiopia at that time was suffocating. Constantly the different factions were trying to recruit you to their side. To remain objective was exhausting, especially as I am not political; after all, I wanted to be a healer.

While at the National Institute of Health, I got the opportunity to go on field trips to two remote parts of the country and spend some time with the indigenous people. One was to the Gambella region in the southwestern corner of the country, and the other one was to Asaita, in the northwestern part of Ethiopia – close to the Danakel depression. The journey to Gambella took a few days on a Toyota land cruiser with my team on board. We passed through difficult terrain and mountainous regions of southwestern Ethiopia, crossing the Baro River before entering the town of Gambella.

While crossing the Baro River, I recalled a story I heard on the radio when I was in high school about an American Peace Core volunteer who was swallowed by a crocodile while swimming in the Baro River. His body was recovered after the crocodile was shot dead. I admit to feeling dread as we made our crossing on the River, even though the local people, Aknuaks, did not hesitate to swim the river. They seem to know instinctively what parts of the river are crocodile-free.

I planned my trip to Gambella after I attended the WHO conference in Congo Brazzaville on treponemal diseases. During the conference, I met my old medical school mentor Peter Perine, who was a conference expert. Peter worked at Naval Medical Research Unit in Addis Ababa when I was a medical student. At the conference, I had a hunch that I should travel to a remote rural region to identify cases of yaws in Ethiopia since no one has reported it. I had to visit several Aknuak villages and examine the children and collect blood samples.

Aknuaks live in small villages scattered all over the region. The land is covered with tropical forest and grassland, and it is home to giraffes, zebras, and elephants. It's an exquisite country, and I enjoyed being there, primarily because the Aknuak people are friendly and cooperative. Children run around without clothes, and even adults shun traditional attire. This helped me in my research because I was able to detect skin lesions that are characteristic of yaws among children in several villages.

During my stay in the Gambella region, I met another research group led by Dr. Awash Teklehaimanot. They were studying and trying to manage the malaria outbreaks. It was a crucial project since so many were dying, especially those who were newcomers to the region, because of the government resettlement program. The situation was out of control. Thousands were expiring. I was horrified, and I held the misguided regime in Addis responsible for so much human misery.

I did not stay long, though – continuing to move around. My other major research trip was to Asaita, located in the northeastern part of Ethiopia close to Danakil depression, which is part of the Rift valley. Traveling was challenging because the whole region had a desert climate. Afar people are nomadic. Those who settle temporarily near a body of water are often infected with bilharziasis (schistosomiasis). My mission was to conduct pilot drug trials to treat cases of schistosomiasis. The Afars are suspicious and are not as friendly as Aknuaks. It was a big change, but at least I gained an appreciation of their culture and living conditions. Nomadic life is grueling, and Mother Nature is merciless.

I worked for two years at the Institutes for Health. Moving from one locale to the next, I spent most of my time thinking and researching. I met many people – many good people – but I did not form any close relationships. Maybe that's why I became convinced that it was time to leave Ethiopia. I had tried on two other occasions to go to the States – and had been denied – but now I decided it was time to go. I started contacting everyone I knew. And I was told, repeatedly, that the government would never let me leave Ethiopia. I resented this deeply. I was sick and tired of being told what I could and could not do. I wanted to be a free man in the worst way – or the best way, I should say.

I continued to communicate with old friends and acquaintances. An idea started to germinate in collaborative research. I initiated a research proposal with Dr. R. E. Shope at Yale, and my proposal was submitted to Fogarty International Center. It was a project that suited me perfectly. Everything I knew would be called into play in this project, and I felt as though I would have a lot to offer. The research proposal was to investigate the situation of arbovirus and hemorrhagic fever viruses in Ethiopia. Hemorrhagic fever viruses include Ebola and yellow fever, among others.

With faculty members of Yale public Health School of medicine; Arbo -Virus Research Unit

I was offered the research opportunity, but the Derg Regime refused to allow me to go. I was enraged. I discussed the matter with the Commissioner of Science, Abebe Muluneh, who happened to be a good friend of mine. He contacted some officials, but he found out that it was a political game because the government had distanced itself considerably from the United States. I appealed again to every politician and professor I knew – pleading with them to give me a chance to further my studies abroad. Again, I was denied.

This went on for three years: requesting permission and being denied. I did not give up. The more the authorities told me to stay put, the more determined I became to leave

Ethiopia. I went to the Minister of Health, General Gizaw Tsehai. When I asked him why I was denied a travel visa, he said, "It is not in support of the revolution." A revolution that ends up keeping an individual in bondage is not a revolution. It is a lie.

I would not rest. I continued petitioning. When I was recognized with an award at the Ethiopian Medical Association Annual Conference, I finally got permission to leave the country. Dr. Getachew Tadesse, vice minister of health, gave me a letter for the Minister of Foreign Affairs so that I could get a passport. A little notoriety had done for me what I could not do for myself, which was get me out of Ethiopia.

There was only one drawback. Before they would give their final approval, I had to assure them that the specimens I had collected had nothing to do with the AIDS epidemic (which they were hiding). I assured them that my research had nothing to do with their secret, and I was allowed to leave. After four years, I finally left for the United States on June 22, 1989.

Chapter 8: A Year of Thirteen Months

Just as i was getting ready to leave Ethiopia in 1989, the revolution almost died. Mengistu was in East Germany when guerrillas and part of the military attempted to depose him. Fighting with tanks and artillery broke out at army barracks on the edge of the capital, Addis Ababa, even though worldwide the coup was being reported as "bloodless." Intense negotiations ensued. It was a precarious time. Everyone wondered who would fill the vacuum left by Mengistu.

I can be singled focused when necessary and when the coup happened, I could only think about one thing: I envisioned my visa to the United States evaporating on the spot.

This was my third opportunity to go to America, and as they say in baseball, three strikes and you're out. If the political upheaval continued, if anything else threatened Mengistu, I was at risk of losing yet another chance to go to America.

And then there was this nagging thought that I was leaving my family behind, even though my father wanted me to go. I knew Mengistu's departure from the government would benefit Ethiopia, but I didn't know when or how. There was a good chance that the country would be thrown into chaos and confusion again. I was sick and tired of the constant turmoil. Political troubles are an impediment to the development of a nation – and an individual. I had reached my saturation point. Without telling anyone, I made the decision to leave Ethiopia for good – no matter what.

As always, I had to remain circumspect about my future – just in case the government changed its mind about allowing me to leave.

The atmosphere in Ethiopia as I finalized my travel arrangements was alarming. I knew something was brewing when Ethiopia's Marxist President, Lieut. Colonel Mengistu Haile Mariam, gave a group of pro-government dignitaries a pep talk and then flew off for a four-day state visit to East Germany. I just didn't realize that within a few hours of Megistu's departure, many senior army officers would instigate a revolt against Mengistu's rigidly Marxist regime.

The attempted coup began when rebel officers seized the Defense Ministry. Major General Haile Giorgis Habte Mariam, the Defense Minister, refused to join the revolt and was killed. Some reports claimed MiG-21s and helicopters were screeching over the capital and tanks and armored personnel carriers converging on the ministry. That all hell had broken loose. Other reports said the coup unfolded almost casually – with troops smoking cigarettes and watching as the action developed, without rancor or bloodshed. Meanwhile, in Asmara, the northern provincial capital and Ethiopia's second largest city, Mengistu's Second

Army, some 150,000 strong, was said to instigate a mutiny. To confuse matters further, in sympathy with the rebellion, the Eritrean People's Liberation Front announced a two-week cease-fire in its 27-year-old war of secession.

Within a day of the coup, Mengistu rushed home to restore control. He cut Ethiopia off from the outside world, closing airports and telecommunications lines. By week's end, the President announced that the coup had failed and vowed that his forces would "liquidate" the traitors. According to the State Ruling Council, most of the conspirators had surrendered. But the toll of the insurrection included nine generals, including the air force commander and the army Chief of Staff. The generals who were killed in Asmara were tortured and mutilated by their own soldiers. These were respected men – highly educated and trained. I knew some of them personally. I met General Regassa Gima when I was in Axum and General Afework Woldemichael when I was the medical director of Tatke Hospital. They were decent men.

Mengistu's Soviet-supplied army was one of the largest and best equipped in Africa, but it suffered what one Ethiopian officer called "disastrous, bloody chaos." The preceding year it was trounced by rebels from the Tigre People's Liberation Front, which had been fighting the government for twelve years. A year earlier, 19,000 government soldiers were beaten by Eritrean forces. These defeats further destabilized Mengistu's reputation.

Army officers claimed they were demoralized by political mishandling of military affairs and by worries of eventual weapons shortages as Moscow pressured Mengistu to settle the civil war. Much of the civilian population wanted to see their leader deposed. I was not the only one reaching a saturation point. People were particularly angered when Mengistu ordered the forced conscription of 100,000 youngsters.

The Derg was finally losing ground; fourteen years of revolution in Ethiopia had taken its toll. While I was relieved that Mengistu was losing his stranglehold on the country, I had no desire to hang around and witness the outcome. The continual eruption of violence had worn me down. I wanted out.

So when the fellowship at Yale was granted, and I received permission to go to America, I secretly planned not to return to Ethiopia – without knowing how I was going to do it. I knew that once I was in America, I would figure out a way to stay. In the meantime, I had to act as if I were just leaving the country for a year. Accordingly, that meant I left Ethiopia with the 1,900 specimens and a little more.

My cousin and his family in Queens met me upon my arrival at JFK airport. The CDC had given me a permit to carry my specimens on board, but until arrangements at Yale could be finalized, my cousin would have to provide a couch in his apartment for me to sleep on and a refrigerator to hold my frozen specimens. My cousin had inquisitively asked:

"What are those?"

"Research specimens human sera," I replied.

"Oh, OK, put them behind the ice cubes then."

My first introduction to this country was not to the teeming masses and endless opportunities. Instead, what struck me about my newly adopted country was how noisy it was. It was July, and music blared from car radios and the streets well past midnight. If I had been younger, I would have probably enjoyed all the commotion because at least it wasn't the sound of gunfire. But I was 37 years old when my plane landed in New York, and the noise was an encumbrance to be endured rather than a seduction. After dealing with the tumult of Ethiopia, I yearned for peace and quiet. I thought I would discover that peace and quiet in New York.

That was a notion that rightfully belongs to the myth that the streets are paved with gold.

I had to go to New Haven to find peace. I thanked my cousin and took a train north to my new home. I stayed for one week at the faculty guest house on campus. After I set up my specimens in the lab – under the tutelage of Dr. Robert

E. Shope – I was shown a studio apartment within walking distance of Yale. I had no money for furniture, so the first night, I slept on a towel on the floor. Soon after, I bought a couch and a television set, but that was as far as my budget would stretch. I had very little money because bringing more than a few hundred would have set off alarm bells at home that I was planning to stay longer, so I contented myself with the bare minimum. It was not luxurious, but I knew there were other comforts that were of greater value to me now that I was in America.

For one, I could now work freely and resolutely without interruption. I was committed to advancing science – to studying arenaviruses, filoviruses, bunyaviruses, and flaviviruses in all their manifestations. With the exception of yellow fever and Argentine hemorrhagic fever, no vaccines had been devised to prevent viral hemorrhagic fevers or VHFs. I was optimistic – and hoping to find a cure or at least contribute to one. I had traveled to the remote areas of Ethiopia, in districts like Gambella, Asaita, Deddesa Valley, so I knew how the people suffered first-hand. I would think about these people when I was alone. I wanted to help them. I wanted to make an impact on their lives. Conceptually, that was my thought and intention then.

To me, there was only one drawback. My fellowship would end in a year, so I did not have all the time in the world.

This looming deadline haunted me for the first few months I was in America. I had a J-1 Visa and not many options. The sword of Damocles hung over my head. It became such a distraction that I was worried it would begin to affect my research, so I joined one of the laboratory scientists in a Bible study group. I was beginning to feel the pangs of loneliness that every immigrant feels during those initial months. The study group helped. I stopped thinking incessantly about whether I should return to Ethiopia or figure out a way to stay in America. Having some companionship after working in the lab all day allowed me to focus on what was in front of me. I settled down, but I was still very conscious of time. And extending time was paramount – my priority.

After a few months, I went to Bethesda to do some testing of my specimens at the military lab there. While in Bethesda, I visited Dr. Wood, a colleague I had worked with in Addis Ababa. He had been my mentor when I was a young man, and I was thrilled when he invited me to share a Thanksgiving dinner with him and his family. I witnessed my first snowfall that Thanksgiving. I stayed at his home, and his wife Nacy and his children Betty and Andy were all loving. I felt at home. I fell in love with the nation called America because of the love of this family. Forever love!

To someone from the Horn of Africa, snow is a spectacle. You see it with the eyes of a child. Glorious. I got so caught up in the moment that I was almost tempted to ask Dr. Wood to intercede on my behalf – to help me figure out a way to stay in America – but I reconsidered. He had helped me so much in my career that I didn't want to burden him with another request – at least right away. In February, we were planning to meet in Hawaii at a conference, and I decided to ask him then. We would be staying at the same hotel and in the same room. I did not do it!

The conference in Hawaii came and went, and I was still unable to ask Dr. Wood for help. I was young, so I could not figure out how to repay those who had done so much for me. I didn't realize that these people weren't looking for repayment. Instead, they were setting an example – hoping that one day I would pass the favors on to those who came after.

Fortunately, I started to make friends in my new country. In fact, I met fellow Ethiopians in Hawaii and began to open up and ask them how to go about obtaining papers to extend my visa. Because of living under a repressive regime, I was very practiced at keeping things to myself. You never knew who would betray you in a country wracked by violence and political upheaval for so many years, so it was a great relief to finally be able to express myself openly. I began to ask a lot of questions.

My one-year fellowship was extended. No one had deported me and put me on a plane back to Ethiopia. When people were surprised to see me after my dreaded one-year deadline, I told my friends I was still in America because I followed the Ethiopian calendar. Like the Coptic calendar, the Ethiopian calendar has twelve months of 30 days each, plus five or six epagomenal days, which comprise a 13th month. This excuse worked for a month. Then 13 months rolled into 14 and 14 months into 15, and 15 months into 16. I continued to buy myself time on a month-to-month basis.

At this point, although I was uncertain about how to proceed, I made the decision that I wanted to pursue my medical career in America. I began to study for the medical exam. Without asking, Dr. Wood gave me a researcher position in the lab at Bethesda, Maryland, and I fell into a peaceful rhythm – studying and working at the lab. I almost forgot about Ethiopia, except when the news came in May 1991 that the Derg had fallen and Mengistu had fled to Zimbabwe. TPL came to power with the support of America. At our meeting at our lab, I expressed my concerns.

I contacted my family and was pleased to find out that they were all safe and sound, despite the changes going on politically. Briefly, I considered returning. I knew things would be different now that the regime had fallen. But then I had to ask myself what I would return to dire economic conditions, drought, famine, and ethnic unrest? I found myself in a classic immigrant dilemma. Although my life in America was not perfect, the threat of returning to my former life was enough to propel me to stay – to take my chances living in America. It still was a land of great promise.

I decided to apply for political asylum. I was denied. I wondered how dire the situation had to become before being granted asylum. Certainly, the last 14 years of my life in Ethiopia provided enough fodder to make a case for asylum. What had to happen to me before the government would consider me a candidate for asylum? It seemed unfair. Luckily, I didn't dwell on this bitterness. Almost by accident, a friend suggested that I investigate the lottery.

I won ... a green card. And it felt like I had won a million dollars.

I passed my medical exam and applied for a residency at Our Lady of Mercy Hospital in the Bronx. My confidence began to grow, and I was convinced that – without all the commotion and upheaval and political strife – I could succeed in this country.

For the third time in three years, I moved yet again; this time to Yonkers, where I got an apartment. My stay in America was beginning to resemble my peripatetic life in Ethiopia – moving from district to district to work and research – constantly in motion. This suited me on so many levels. Constant movement was in my genes. I could cope well with new places and new faces. In many ways, it allowed me to stay in my head. I did not have to master the challenges of close ties. That was a benefit. But on another level, America was the antithesis to Ethiopia. There was stability here – opportunity and abundance.

Once the threat of being deported to Ethiopia evaporated, I could concentrate on my career – without the distractions of torture, war, and revolution. To be able to study in earnest – to focus on the things that mattered to me deeply – was a joy. It is very disabling to always be looking over your shoulder and to have to cope with the violent loss of friends and associates on a regular basis. All this suffering takes up a lot of psychic space in the head. More than a million people died during the civil unrest in Ethiopia from 1974 to 1991. I considered myself extremely fortunate to be alive and starting a new life in America.

Chapter 9: Gamachu

More than 80 ethnic groups reside in Ethiopia, with the largest being the Oromo – the roots of my family – followed by the Amhara. In its own way, Ethiopia is diverse. Cultures and traditions bump and clash – sometimes detrimentally and sometimes advantageously.

When Meles Zenawi came to power in 1991 after the Derg was deposed, Meles formed a multi-party system, EPRDF (Ethiopian People's Revolutionary Democratic Front). The Tigray ethnic group, which constitutes about 6 percent of the population, maintains most of the key positions – much to the consternation of the Amhara's and Oromos (about 60 percent of the population). But, even though there continues to be discontent regarding the government, at least this government is an improvement on the devastation wreaked by the Derg regime. Progress was slowly being made in education and health – and economic growth was declared, but economists argue that it was fake. Most of the aid money was siphoned out of the country by the ruling group.

The diversity of Ethiopia, with all its tribes, traditions, and languages, was good preparation for what I found in the melting pot of America – New York. You can rub elbows with every nationality in New York. I rarely felt like an outsider walking down the streets of the city. Coming from

Ethiopia, the animated conversations and disputes of all the different nationalities in New York felt almost familiar. All these competing ideas and beliefs create vibrancy and dynamics that make a community stronger. And a consensus reached after hammering it out is inevitably stronger than an unexamined settlement.

I think this is one of the reasons why I was so surprised – and unhappy – during my residency at Our Lady of Mercy Medical Center in the Bronx. A friend of mine, Fassil Tefera, suggested to me at that time that there was an opening at Our Lady of Mercy Medical Center. He was in his third year in the residency program, and I decided to apply. Fassil had always been supportive, and I liked the idea of knowing someone while I struggled through my first year. Like so many third-year residents, he was extremely busy, so I had to figure out a lot on my own – a good thing in the end. While we shared many experiences and common values, I had to fend for myself. (Dr. Fassil Tefera and I are lifelong friends.)

When I got to the medical center in the Bronx, I had expected a typically diverse New York environment where I could work hard and move ahead. Instead, I found myself in a suffocating program where, for the most part, I felt underutilized yet overworked. Because of the lack of standards, Our Lady of Mercy was anything but a learning atmosphere.

The Chief of Medicine, the doctor responsible for recruiting residents, was a highly capable doctor and master teacher. Except for a few residents, I and another resident from Ghana, Adolfe Nyarko, Dr. Pitchumoni recruited only residents who came from India. Some of us thought it was a closed circle.

I will admit there is something to be said for recruiting like-minded people – many organizations and companies recruit this way – but this situation went beyond like-mindedness. Dr. Pitchumoni instead created an exclusive circle of residents who merely parroted his ideas and work ethic without question. This can be disastrous in a hospital setting – were life and death jockeys for supremacy daily. While I liked him personally, and he was a master teacher and scientist, it was not a good situation.

I was living in Yonkers at the time, and the long hours were grinding, but I could have tolerated this. Lack of sleep and stress are not uncommon in the lives of medical residents. What was disturbing, though, was that I had very little interaction with my colleagues. For the first time in my life in America, I felt like an outsider. The administrators at the hospital were not interested in my ideas, nor were they willing to share learning opportunities that were more challenging than the daily slop work residents often get thrown their way. I felt side-lined – as did the other resident from Ghana – and often helpless when low standards or severe understaffing created crisis situations for the patients.

I was deeply frustrated. Part of it had to do with the fact that I was unable to demonstrate my skills as a physician. I had come from a crisis in war-torn Ethiopia – and I had been given a great deal of responsibility there – and now I was relegated to know-nothing status at this poorly run hospital in the Bronx. I began fantasizing about getting out of there as soon as possible and started looking into academic opportunities that would allow me to exit without jeopardizing my career. I realized later that it was not about my desire to do what I think is right but about integrating into the system obediently.

In the meantime, I had to grin and bear the grueling schedule. After a few months of being repeatedly dismissed for offering my opinions, I decided to take a different approach. During my daily rounds, I told myself, "When in Rome, do as the Romans do." Basically, I learned how to keep things to myself, which was not difficult for me since I was practiced at keeping my own counsel because of my experience in Ethiopia. In all fairness to the other residents – even those within the circle – I knew most of them were not exactly thrilled with the conditions at Our Lady of Mercy.

We were on call for long hours, and there were instances where patients died due to medical errors that resulted from physical and mental fatigue – that happened at a lot of hospitals. One night, Kanagala, who is still a good friend, was assigned to the intensive medical unit as an on-call resident while I was on a regular medical unit. He came running to me at 5 a.m. in the morning, trembling and shaking. He was unable to complete drawing blood on 10 of the ICU patients that he had taken care of that night. He wanted my help … immediately. Luckily, I was able to assist. It was common knowledge that the chief of the ICU would lash into him if he didn't complete his duties in a timely manner. And God help Kanagala if anyone died; as a result, his inability to take care of everyone at once. Every intern had already suffered these humiliations in the program.

Fear is an enemy. It hinders learning. It creates misery. As a result of the leadership at Our Lady of Mercy, some residents who were not part of the inner circle left for other opportunities at different hospitals.

Most of the time, I felt isolated, frustrated, or tired – not the right frame of mind when dealing with patients. To counteract this malaise – to find some solace in an unhappy situation – I started dating a nurse. I met her in the medical unit.

Susan was born in Jamaica (a mix of Jamaican and Portuguese), and she has a light complexion and a fiery spirit. We dated for a month. The attraction was mutual, even though we were opposite in so many ways. I was hoping she would help me forget what I had to do day in, day out at the hospital. That was a mistake. It is never a good idea to seek escape in another human being. Susan and I began to argue – a little at first, then more and more. We broke up after dating for a few months.

Now I felt totally alone. I was even morose. I had to shake myself out of it before I made a rash decision – go home to Ethiopia. It took me a few weeks, but I became determined to detach from my residency program and began to rethink my game plan. It's true that I wanted to escape, but I was going to make sure that this time I was going to something more productive than another relationship that filled me with sorrow.

I interviewed for a neurology training program in Pittsburgh. The interview went well, but I decided against it after some thought. I wasn't eager to set up shop again in another completely foreign city. By chance, a Geriatric Fellowship Program had been initiated at Our Lady of Mercy Medical Center. Two doctors had already enrolled. It was intriguing, especially since I began to realize I had a rapport with my older patients.

When the program director began to persuade me to enroll as the second opportunity came around, I was flattered. My initial medical goal was to work for the World Health Organization in infectious disease. I even met the

WHO chief of virology when I attended the Tropical Medicine Conference in 1991 in Honolulu while I was at Yale. The WHO chief also encouraged me. I felt some conflict about abandoning my first love. But misery in my current situation at Our Lady of Mercy inevitably began to eat away at my resolve. I applied for the geriatrics program and was accepted.

I liked it immediately. I was able to demonstrate my skills and function to the best of my abilities, which I was unable to do in the residency program, where initiative and know-how were discouraged. I also liked my elderly patients very much and enjoyed teaching residents. I gave presentations at Grand Rounds and got a warm reception. I thought about embarking on an academic career. I was finally getting some acknowledgment for all the work I was doing in the Geriatric Fellowship – and I liked it. I became a member of the American Geriatric Society (AGS) and became further involved.

Although the Geriatrics Program director was not exactly pleased, I attended the AGS annual conference in Atlanta in 1997. After the last few months, I knew I needed a boost of some sort – and learning had always been a healthy pursuit for me. I petitioned the director until I was granted permission, and I flew to Atlanta for the conference paying my own expenses while fellows from other centers were supported by their programs. It was one of my best decisions.

First, I finally found myself among colleagues who were engaged and excited by their career choices and possibilities. The drudgery of medicine was absent from their frame of reference, and that kind of enthusiasm is contagious – in a very good way.

I was finally feeling invigorated by my profession.

Normally the geriatrics specialty is a one-year or a two-year program, but I had to opt for the one-year program because I received some unexpected news. Although we had only dated for a month, Susan contacted me and told me she was pregnant.

I am human, and I must admit I found it easier delivering shocking news to my patients than it was for me to digest this bit of information from my intimate friend. First, I am organized, and a conscientious planner and this event definitely put a kink in my elaborate strategies. My reaction? I was sullen at first – disbelieving – until Susan came by my apartment with the sonogram in her hand to show me a picture of the sprouting baby.

I softened. And the more I thought about it, more I softened. I told Susan I would be a committed father … forever. Susan was happy.

Until she became progressively sicker and sicker during her first trimester, I was worried about her, so we agreed that I should leave my Yonkers apartment and move in with her in Pomona, New York. Susan had two children, a boy, and a girl, from a previous marriage, so it was quite an adjustment for this bachelor. I had suddenly inherited a family. I had to learn very quickly how to jockey family and the fellowship – without losing my balance and going over the deep end. It was not easy.

But the fellowship did vastly improve my standing at Our Lady of Mercy Medical Center. For one, I was no longer treated poorly. I was amazed how a title – I was now a medical fellow – could shift the perspectives of even the most recalcitrant and disrespectful residents. My working life was no longer such a burden. I began to teach and instruct – and I made sure that I did it without intimidating and belittling the new residents.

While I was busy preparing reports on clinical and laboratory research work, instructing medical and technical staff, keeping statistics on patient treatments, and attending conferences, staff meetings, and seminars in geriatrics, my son was gestating in Susan's womb. I am a doctor, but I still think of birth as a miraculous event.

Despite my awe, though, the night Susan went into labor, I had just finished a double shift. I brought her to the hospital. I checked all her vitals. I conferred with the staff and attending doctor at the local hospital. It would be a while before the baby was born. That's when I told Susan I had to go home and catch a few winks of sleep. Susan was not happy.

Somehow, I managed to rationalize my decision to go home. What good would I be if I were bleary-eyed and incoherent from lack of sleep? I pulled the covers over my head and slept fitfully. I thought Susan was making too big of a fuss about my leaving her. I am not a fan of the drama of any kind. Still, I felt I needed to defend myself. I reverted to my experience in Ethiopia, where women go through childbirth stoically – often without medical care – trying to assuage my guilt. I still couldn't sleep, so I sheepishly returned to the hospital feeling exhausted but with growing sympathy for how my wife must be feeling in comparison. When I got to the delivery room, Susan's mood had worsened. She was spitting mad. All I can say is I am a fortunate man that I made it back to that hospital just before the baby was born.

Gamachu was born on April 16, 1997. I was blessed by God that day. My son's name means "the bringer of joy and happiness." It was my grandfather's name – the one who fought against the Italians at Maychew. My grandfather was a hero in our family as well as our community. I decided to name my son after him. I love the name.

When I was in high school, I wanted to change my own name to my grandfather's. Now I had a chance to name my own son after him. It felt entirely wonderful to have a son. And Gamachu did not disappoint. He was – and is – perfect in every way.

Gamachu when he was 2 years old

Chapter 10: Hale Luya

When gamachu was 3 years old in 1999, I decided he was old enough to meet my family in Ethiopia. More than 16 hours on a plane is a challenge for a little guy (not to mention a big guy). I didn't know if Gamachu would pine for Susan right away or start fidgeting and complaining and driving the other passengers crazy, but I decided to take a chance. My father and Tigist were growing older. I was exceedingly proud of my son, and I had not been back to Ethiopia in more than ten years, so I was missing my family and country too.

Gamachu, the bringer of joy, more than lived up to his name. He was full of wonder at the whole experience and immediately made friends with my family – even the large crowd waiting for us at the airport – my father, Tigist, my sister, and cousins, cousins, cousins.

It was a wonderful homecoming. Ethiopians are hospitable and good-natured, which is remarkable considering the troubles they've seen. The country had changed considerably since I had left. Ten years later, I was relieved to find that – internally, at least – it was without strife and moving forward – inch by inch. A war with Eritrea had claimed almost 70,000 lives, but that, too, was finally over in 1999. Ethiopia had claimed victory in that war, and a shaky peace had settled between the neighboring nations. Eritrea was part of Ethiopia when I left for the US in 1989.

Because I have such a large, extended family, Gamachu and I stayed at a hotel in Addis rather than with my father and Tigist. Although my son loved playing with all his cousins, I knew he would need a reprieve every now and then. We would be there for two weeks, and I had to attend a conference for a few days, so it would be better if I had a quiet place for him to stay while a cousin watched him. It was a whirlwind of activity.

After paying my respects to my family and eating several noisy, sumptuous meals, I took a ride to the western section of Addis, where I lived, prior to moving to the States. The country may have been going through enormous change and upheaval, but I still have fond memories of this little area in Addis, which I spent a good deal of time in just before I came to the United States. Personally and professionally, I was doing well back then. I had just finished collecting my specimens, and I was working at the hospital to save money before going to America. I don't know what motivated me at that time, but I decided to open a private practice – figuring I had already waited a few years for a visa, and who knew if I could end up waiting another few years for the government to give me permission to leave the country – if they ever did.

I opened the Hale Luya Clinic, which I would race to after finishing all my other duties of the day. Thinking about the name of the clinic, I suppose I was feeling joyous in

1987, knowing I had a future ahead of me (hopefully in America) and knowing deep in my bones too that Ethiopia was about to take a turn for the better now that the Derg's influence was fizzling. The clinic attracted patients immediately, and even a few local companies began to send their workers to me as well for general medical care. I thoroughly enjoyed tending to my patients on an individual basis. For the first time in my medical career, everything was not an emergency or crisis, and I was developing relationships with my patients. Besides knowing what ailed them, I knew how many children they had, where they worked, how they managed to survive even during the difficult years.

When I returned ten years later with my son, I returned to the old neighborhood where I lived in a spacious apartment and had started the Hale Luya clinic. It is now a bustling business district. The clinic is no longer there, but a doctor friend's wife, a woman who had grown up in this section of the Ethiopian capital, told me when we were having dinner at her home in New York that a small section in western Addis the area where the clinic was located, is now known as the Hale Luya. I was happy to have left something of a legacy in my country of origin.

In many respects, the name of the clinic was a harbinger of things to come. I called it the Hale Luya Clinic because, at that time, I knew there were more components to wellness than physical health. The word Hallelujah appears in the Book of Psalms, and its literal translation is to join in praise to God. I felt even then that there was a spiritual element to good health – sometimes neglected in Western medicine – and I wanted to emphasize this to my patients. In 1989, anyone who had survived the last 25 years in Ethiopia had a lot to be grateful for; we needed to celebrate life and health. We needed to take a closer look at the things that matter to us – besides who was in power and who was out.

The Hale Luya Clinic, as short-lived as it was, obviously had had an impact on the old neighborhood. That was encouraging because back home in the States, I was on the verge of opening a new private practice – considering the location, discussing it with a potential partner, and figuring out the financial ins and outs. I had the feeling that if I could make it work in Ethiopia, I had a good shot of getting it done in New York. Still, I was having such a wonderful time in Ethiopia that I didn't want to go home, even though the conference was over and I had visited with all my relatives. I decided to stay a third week.

It did not go over too well with Susan. She complained that she was missing Gamachu, which surprised me because I felt as though I was giving her a little peace from a 3-year-old and allowing her more time to spend with her two other children, Jonathan and Natasha. I was having difficulty pleasing Susan, and it bothered me. I was 40 years old, so I didn't want to answer someone else for my actions. But, on another level, I was probably also postponing the inevitable by staying another week. As soon as I got home, I knew I was going to have to put all my plans for a private practice into action – and that was a little intimidating. Going into private practice is more complicated than it seems.

I was used to collecting a salary. After I finished my fellowship, I began working at the Jewish Home and Hospital in the Bronx in my specialty of geriatrics. Also, once the director of the hospital found out that I had spent a good deal of time studying infectious diseases, I was put in charge of a research program. In addition, I made extra money by moonlighting in the emergency room at the local hospital, so now, with a private practice, I was jumping into the unknown – unsure of my income but not my skills. Luckily money was never the driving force in practicing medicine. Of course, I wanted enough to pay my bills and take care of my family, but I was more concerned about the well-being of my patients and offering a service than I was about becoming rich.

I am a firm believer that abundance comes from being happy at what you do. As the Buddha once said, "Success is not the key to happiness. Happiness is the key to success. If you love what you are doing, you will be successful."

I was fortunate because if I had been more focused on becoming rich than offering patient satisfaction and attending to my responsibilities, I probably would never have done what I did. I looked for a practice in the Bronx. I wanted to share the space with Dr. Duge, another doctor from the Jewish Home and Hospital who already had a family practice in Long Island. After a few months of searching and considering various locations, we finally started a practice. Because it took us some time to get the office up and running, we did not inherit any of the former doctor's patients because they had already been reassigned to different doctors.

Luckily, I am good at organization, so we did not have to struggle long to find new patients. During the initial few months, I was still at the Jewish Home and Hospital, so I managed to acquire quite a few patients from my work at the hospital, and I continued to work at the local emergency room to ensure that I had the income to cover all the myriad costs associated with opening our own practice. Patients seemed to come to us organically, and we were eventually able to detach ourselves from our former positions at the hospitals.

New business adventures are invigorating but also exhausting. Every business owner will tell you how a new business will consume your every waking hour during those first few years. We were no exception. I spent 12 to 14 hours a day getting the practice in place – and trying to keep up with all the new innovations and research in my field.

Gamachu was just a baby, so I sometimes feel as though I missed many moments in those formative years – even though I made every effort to be an involved parent and father.

I was happy though, in my career. The work has a way of directing you – the cycle grabs you and pushes you in the direction that you need to go. I would wake up each morning excited about the day ahead of me and the patients I would see. I made enjoyment of my work the bottom line – not the money I was making. Of course, I had those moments when I questioned why I had abandoned my initial goal of becoming infectious diseases expert– like a journalist who daydreams about the great American novel still swimming in his head – but these thoughts would disappear once I got to the office. My patients became a priority, and I became more and more enthused by my ability to help them recover and improve their lives. Although I love my books and am deeply interested in research, I am, at the core of my being, a people person.

And it was challenging to practice in the Bronx. For the most part, my patients were older, but eventually, I began to focus on wellness issues – things like weight management in particular – and my patient base began to broaden. While my geriatric patients are considerate, respectful, and compliant, my younger patients – many on Medicaid – began to defy me in ways I was not accustomed to. I had to become creative in getting them to buy into compliance, even though I could not figure out why anyone would go to the doctor and then ignore the doctor's directions and guidance.

Another trend that impacted my practice – and every other doctor's practice in America during the last decade – was the profound shift insurance companies began to have on medical care. Like so many other doctors, I began to resent their interference. Instead of spending more time on patient care, we were forced to comply with the insurance companies' excessive regulations. I found myself getting caught up in paperwork – not to mention rigorous authorizations and complicated drug formularies – and I was diverted from what really mattered: fostering my patients' good health. Not to mention that I have been dealing with more and more uninsured – and noncompliant patients – during the last few years.

It was frustrating, but in a way, it drove me in a direction that I find more and more appealing. I chose to head toward wellness as opposed to symptom-based medicine. It began to make more sense to me to intervene in the patient's health before the disease occurred, so I started to promote good nutrition and exercise before the patient became obese and presented with diabetes. I hired a part-time nutritionist. My diagnosis focused on preventative measures patients could take when they were heading toward a bad outcome – from smoking or obesity, or lack of exercise.

Although I am awed by the possibilities of Western medicine, wellness – rather than holistic medicine (I would not send a patient to an acupuncturist for acid reflux) – has become, more and more, the focus of my practice. In fact, I plan to eventually open a Wellness Clinic, where the whole person is examined and diagnosed – their physical, mental, spiritual, and emotional health – so that we can properly guide them in the right direction of graceful and healthful aging. I would like to see more of my patient's become advocates for their own health by practicing good habits of nutrition and exercise - becoming proactive by helping them get involved in Tai Chi or yoga. I look at the 21st Century as a time when the East will truly meet the West on an equal footing – and we will all be better off as a result.

It is an exciting time to practice medicine because we are on the tipping point of a new way of thinking and practicing. The new healthcare initiative will have a significant impact on how we practice medicine during the next 50 years. That's why, during the last five years, my hospital-based practice has not been neglected. In fact, more than 50 percent of my patients are hospital-based. (In the Bronx, primarily because I specialize in geriatrics, I have the distinction of the most admissions among solo practitioners.) I served as a member of the executive board of Montefiore Medical Center, where we, unfortunately, had to spend a good deal of time determining the patients' length of stay in the hospital because of reimbursement issues dictated by the insurance companies. Without a doubt, the process of healthcare reform is a complicated matter.

Everybody agrees that there is a need for reform, but how this will play out is a matter of conjecture. Like so many other doctors, I have enjoyed the lively debate, which was full of surprises. Why the Democrats voted against the bill that limits malpractice lawyers while the Republicans voted against the salaries of CEOs of health insurance is anyone's guess. But there were a lot of stakes, namely, patients' health and a doctor's ability to practice medicine in the way he or she was trained. The jury is still out on the new health care bill, but we must all become invested in the best outcome – for everyone involved. However, change is inevitable.

Chapter 11: My Father's Shade

Gamachu at an age of 3 and his dog Sassi.

July was hot, but my father said that 80 degrees F was mild in comparison to Ethiopia. He said that the heavy hot air in Newark felt like springtime. I laughed. I was glad to see him. When I had visited him in Ethiopia two years earlier, I had told him we must not wait another ten years before visiting each other again, and I made him promise that he would plan a trip to New York to stay with me and Gamachu. He had not been feeling well for the past six months, and I felt a deep need to see him. I picked my father up at Newark Airport.

He was excited because he was finally going to meet Susan and see my home and practice. My father had never tried to influence any of my career decisions. His life had centered on the farm at Tulu Mara, agriculture, building schools, maneuvering the assaults of the Derg, and fostering his government appointments. But because he valued education, I knew he was proud of me. And it was obvious right there in the car. He was full of questions and looked happy sitting in the front seat of my 1991 Mercedes.

My father kept looking out the car window and commenting on all the trees lining Route 287 on our way to the Tappan Zee Bridge. The trees impressed him deeply. I knew why he found them so seductive. Ethiopia had suffered massive deforestation during the last quarter century. My memories as a child abound with forests and green farmland, but right before my eyes, those forests and lush highlands disappeared. Now only 3 percent of the land in Ethiopia has the benefit of shade (instead of 40 percent coverage 100 years ago).

The government in the late '70s claimed it was the farmer's fault, which flies in the face of scientific and United

Nations research as well as my own experience. Based on Soviet and Chinese models, the Derg forcibly confiscated land from individual owners and turned those acres into state-owned farmland. Because the small farmer was displaced and ownership of the land was no longer fiercely protected, the land was abused beyond repair. No one protected the trees. Forests were cleared for livestock pastures and for farmland focused on exporting commodity crops (coffee, tea, and sesame), or the wood was used for charcoal fuel – without any attention toward soil erosion, aridity, extinction of animals, or the displacement of native populations. Population growth has not helped matters either.

Today no land is owned privately in Ethiopia. Instead, the land is leased to foreign investors; countries such as Saudi Arabia, India, and Singapore. My father experienced this shift from private ownership to collective farming personally – feeling it materially when he lost Tulu Mara and psychically when he was imprisoned. I already knew how he felt about the trees and his farm, but as I drove toward my home in upstate New York, I felt his loss – Ethiopia's loss as well – on another level.

I knew he was thinking that in his lifetime, he would never again see the trees restored in Ethiopia. For him, the shade in Ethiopia would remain a fond but vague memory. I prayed it would not be my experience. I am hoping the

Ethiopian government will listen to the people: according to a recent survey, more than 90 percent of the farming community would prefer if the land was privatized again – to ensure that reforestation occurs. I would like to see that happen in my lifetime.

When we pulled up to my house, I expected my father to be impressed by my home. Instead, his initial reaction was that he was impressed by the … trees. It was all he could talk about. It took me a while before I could change the topic. Luckily his family is as important to him as our natural resources. I explained to him we would be getting together with relatives from Canada – the first time for me – who had heard that he was visiting. We were planning a large reunion, and he was the guest of honor, but we had to take care of a few things first.

My father had some medical issues that needed attending to, so we took him on the rounds of doctors that I knew professionally and personally until he eventually ended up, by coincidence, with Dr. Camachu. The doctor felt familiar to both of us – maybe because his name resembled our family name and my son's. Somehow when my father received the diagnosis of severe anemia, due to myelofibrosis, the news wasn't quite so hard to handle coming from this friendly Hispanic doctor's mouth.

I had managed to talk my father into spending more than a month with us. He was reluctant, but I said the trip was too long to turn around and head right back. He agreed – partly because he was very much enamored by America. Besides the trees, he said he felt secure and protected – and he marveled at how manageable life was in the States. We would talk most evenings after I came home from the office – about our friends in Ethiopia; the ones who had passed away; the political upheaval while I was attending school; the farm; his new farm, which was a collection of a few cows and not much more; the new government.

After all those conversations, I, too, would come away with a new appreciation for my life in the States. Gratitude can be contagious. Somehow, I had forgotten how difficult it could be to eke out a living and sustain oneself in Ethiopia. I had put all the storm and strife and political unrest out of my mind. The United States had been very good to me.

He was 83 years old, so he did not have many requirements as far as being entertained went. He walked around the property, ate heartily, and napped. I would go to work, then return home in the evening to find my father relaxed and happy after a day spent in my backyard or accompanying Susan and Gamachu as she drove around. We would eat a nice meal and then talk for the rest of the evening. I was very happy to have my father staying with us. He put little demands on my time but stirred something deep in me – my family ties, my love of Ethiopia and the United States, and my utter respect for him.

One morning I had to visit my Manhattan office. As I was driving south on Major Deegan, the news report on NPR said a helicopter had hit the World Trade Center. It was 8:46 a.m., and I was stuck in bumper-to-bumper traffic. No one was going anywhere. I glanced at my watch and realized I would never make it to the office in time to see my patients, so I turned around. It was a gorgeous September morning with the sun shining and the sky brilliant blue, and I did not feel like getting stuck on Major Deegan for three hours, so instead, I headed back to Montefiore Hospital in the Bronx, where I could attend to my other duties.

By the time I arrived at the hospital, everyone was in a state of shock. It was apparent that it wasn't a helicopter at all. I went to the doctor's lounge, where my colleagues were glued to the television. Just as I sat down to watch, another plane went crashing into the other tower of the WTC at 9:03 a.m. We looked at one another in disbelief. You could see each of the doctors do a mental calculation in their heads – trying to figure out who they knew would be in those buildings that morning and at that time. Luckily no one present had loved ones in the building, and we were all able to gather our innards together if this catastrophe became worse than our wildest nightmares.

In the corridors of the hospital, it was a different story. People were in shock or yelling and running, obviously worried and concerned about people they knew who worked at the World Trade Centers.

It is impossible to describe how we all processed the unexpected, except you could see the agony on the faces of each of the doctors, men and women who faced life-or-death situations daily. Their cool, calm exterior melted away visibly on September 11. Just as we were determining what our course of action would be, another commotion occurred around 9:45. A plane had struck the Pentagon. Now we all became frozen in our seats – bracing ourselves for the worst.

My father during his visit to the USA.

It was one thing to witness New York going down, but the prospect that our government was now under attack sent shudders through the room. Immediately every one of us picked up our cell phones – only to find they still didn't work but hoping that the earlier dysfunction had been corrected.

No one in the room had a working cell, so we got in line to use the two landlines in the room and started calling our families. I was waiting and watching the television set simultaneously until a nurse rushed in and asked me to check on a patient in the intensive care ward. I was almost glad to have my attention diverted.

I kept on asking myself what the next best move would be. Should I go to Ground Zero or stay put and attend to my responsibilities here? I truly didn't know what the best course of action was; no one did. There were too many conflicting reports that morning. In many respects, this day reminded me of the day we were under siege at the hospital in Aksum, except no one was accompanying me to the basement and telling me to stay put. For that, I was grateful.

As soon as I dealt with my patient in intensive care, I hurried back to the doctor's lounge, the television, to get a better sense of what was going on. By now, we had heard about the plane that was diverted from the Capitol that had instead gone down in a field in Pennsylvania because the crew and passengers fought off the terrorists. What was worse, though, was that the south tower had collapsed by 10 in the morning. I hadn't been watching the television at that time, but now I couldn't pull myself away from it. A half-hour later, the second tower collapsed. We were shaken to the core; some of us were crying. I met a friend who is a cardiologist named Daniel Levy, in the hospital corridor, and he expressed the situation as the third world war.

To make matters worse, if they could possibly go in that direction, we did not know what to expect next. Nearly 18,000 people worked in the WTC, and according to the Port Authority, nearly 15,000 passes through the lower levels each morning at 8:45 to go to work. The casualties could be overwhelming. We started making a crisis assessment – and, between glimpses of the television and sporadic reports from hospital personnel – we mapped out a strategy for Montefiore Hospital for the next few days. The day became a blur of activity.

Because my cell was still out of order, it was hours before I called my home and let everyone know I was all right. My family was alarmed. I spoke to my father briefly and told him I would probably see him later that evening. He gave me his blessing, and I hunkered down with my colleagues for the long day and night ahead of us. I managed to get home that night – much to everyone's relief.

The rest, of course, is history. A total of 2,995 people lost their lives on the day of the attacks – with more than 90 countries losing citizens. The worst of September 11 was when people began to jump. I understand nearly 200 people jumped from those burning towers. I watched it on the television – horrified. Like so many other New Yorkers, I didn't sleep well that night, but I reported to duty the following morning to St. Vincent's Hospital – not the one in Greenwich Village but the one located in midtown. We handled the overflow of patients who were diverted from the downtown hospitals, so again another day passed in a blur. It was surreal because no one was sure that the worst was over.

My father and I talked about religious extremism and what was happening in East Africa. He seemed to understand it better than I did, but we were too close to the attacks, so everyone and everything was suspect. Islam was the fastest-growing religion in Ethiopia, so we were unable to separate the good from the bad. We berated the Saudi Government for taking over our mining industry and moving so many Muslims into the lowlands of our country. I don't think anyone could see clearly that first week after the attack. We all felt so powerless and angry. We were very emotional. The television coverage of the event tore our hearts apart. My father kept saying to me that 9-11 was the "work of the Devil himself." As I looked at the footage on the television screen, I agreed with him.

To change the subject from Muslims, because it was not healthy for us to become obsessed with their role in the attacks, we spoke about the new land grab in Ethiopia – where foreign investors (American Conglomerates included) were vying for big pieces of the pie in our country to start agribusinesses – as though Ethiopians themselves didn't have a clue what needed to be done. The state of the world hung heavy on our conversations during his stay that summer and fall. I have managed to veer away from politics my whole life, but I felt as though I was getting sucked into it by the recent course of events. You couldn't be in New York at that time and ignore what was going on with the world. That's all we could talk about while he was here.

My father stayed two more months after the WTC devastation. Like so many others, he was queasy about flying, and the airlines were a mess. Every day the regulations changed. Delays were commonplace. When I accompanied him to the airport, I noted how strong, how functional, and how energetic he was for an 83-year-old man. I felt sorry that he had to witness the attacks, but in another respect, I was glad he was here with me. We provided each other comfort at least – and it is always much better to go through a crisis with your family by your side. He had certainly witnessed his own devastation in his lifetime; I was glad that this time we came out unscathed – at least physically.

A few months later, Tigist died after getting anesthesia for a minor injury. I was appalled that this had happened, but there was nothing I could do from my medical office in the Bronx. Tigist had been such a powerful figure in my life – full of so much love and acceptance – at a time when we were all aching for a woman's tender care. I would miss her, but I knew even more that my father would suffer her loss greatly.

Soon after, my father fell ill again. I went back to Ethiopia to straighten out his affairs and help him in the last months of his life. Taking care of a loved one is vastly different than taking care of the patients. My heart ached the entire time I was in Ethiopia. For the life of me, I could not determine what was harder to handle: my father's demise or what had occurred on September 11. Both events were tearing me apart.

I attended to my father the best I could, trying to make him comfortable and trying to reconcile myself to the inevitable. The whole year blurred into a big pocket of pain for me. He died six months after the attacks, just after he turned 84. He was buried at St Michael's church in Bako. Thousands attended the funeral proceedings, some on horseback in line with Oromo tradition. I still miss him.

Chapter 12: The Pull of Politics

An old friend, Mogus Brook, called me in the fall of 2004. He is Ethiopian, but he had emigrated and settled in Pasadena, California, and at that time, he was working for the city of Los Angeles as an engineer. I was surprised to hear from him. I had lost touch many years ago, but almost immediately, Mogus began talking about the upcoming "free" election in Ethiopia – as though we had just had a conversation about the topic yesterday.

I tried to tell Mogus that I had managed to stay apolitical my whole life, and I wanted it to stay that way, but he was a very convincing man. He kept on repeating, "This is a landmark election for Ethiopia." I did not have all my facts, which was evident during our conversation, so I basically listened to him.

After we hung up, I wondered how he managed to get me to pledge a donation. I was, after all, uninterested in politics, especially Ethiopia's. I had too many bitter and painful memories of what had happened to me when I was a student, and the government closed the university. I had lost time – and, even worse, I had lost friends who were ruthlessly murdered by the Derg.

Still, Mogus stirred something in me. I had to admit I had some unresolved feelings to my experience of Ethiopia's political turmoil of the 70s … maybe I could work all these feelings out intellectually. In the 70s I was not fully aware of the black panther's movement in America with a struggle for democracy. Ethiopia needs a democratic government rather than ethnocentric rule by a minority group. At the very least, I was determined to at least familiarize myself with the situation in my country of origin so I could have an intelligent conversation with my friends about what was going on there. I started to do my research – with the same enthusiasm that I approached my studies, medical research, and practice. I began to read everything I could get my hands on that had to do with Ethiopia's upcoming election in 2005. It stirred up a lot of feelings that I thought I had worked out long ago. The idea of the election has brought a positive feeling to me. I still remember the dash days when Haile Selassie's high-ranking officials were massacred by the Derg in 1974. That was a sad moment in the history of the nation when the rule of law was ignored, and lawlessness became the symbol of a nation in the name of revolution. That was a nation that fought for world peace as a leading member of the League of Nations and then a founding member of the United Nations.

    The general election in Ethiopia was going to be held on May 15, 2005. Seats in the national as well as nine regional government councils were up for grabs. Because I am Oromo by birth, I was familiar with the legitimate complaints Oromos – and the other ethnic groups – had about the Ethiopian government. Prime Minister Meles Zenawi, a Tigran, and his cohorts, had been in power too long. They monopolized the government, and most of the Ethiopian people were fed up. There was rampant ethnic divisiveness, and too many groups were under-represented. Finally, with pressure from the outside world, the government was arm-twisted into holding a democratic election. I would have scoffed at the idea of a free election, except those observers from the Carter Center and European Union would be on board to make sure that the results were not tainted. I was hopeful. Maybe something positive would happen if the international community got involved.

I was surprised at how quickly I was consumed by what was going on in Ethiopia. It felt as though I was reliving my past – from a safe distance – and experiencing my frustration all over again. As an American, I think it's difficult to comprehend how stable and manageable our lives are because we have a democratic system in place – full of checks and balances. You can organize your life without too much outside interference. And better yet, power shifts continually in the United States – even if it's just from one party to the next. Now, when I think of January 6, 2020, resurrection to overturn an election in the US, I think of how democracy is vulnerable in a nation that advocates democracy so that a psychopath like Donald Trump can bring darkness and destroy democratic values.

That is not the case in Third World countries, especially countries in Africa. Although we get glimpses of unmanageability in other countries – the devastating earthquake in Haiti comes to mind – the daily chaos and suffering remain far removed from our consciousness. Most Americans still put their heads down on a soft pillow at night, with their bellies full and their personal safety intact. Life is not perfect here (many are still healing from 9-11 and Hurricane Katrina), but for the most part, Americans are certain they will have electricity in the morning to get their coffee brewed; they know there's a desk in the public schools for their children; they know the streets will be plowed so they can hurry off to their jobs after the snow falls. And, ultimately, we know if we don't like something, we can go to the election booth and cast our votes to make a change – without looking down the barrel of a gun. We sometimes take this for granted.

So, all this was going through my head as I studied the 2005 election in Ethiopia. I felt energized by the new developments. The Coalition for Unity and Democracy Party was mobilizing. This group, which included myriad opposition parties to the government, was planning a peaceful demonstration in Addis Ababa. It's a great benefit when you can study something – observe it objectively – without intimidation. I was not allowed to do this when I was a university student as many of my friends at that time were "disappearing" left and right. During the 70s, when I was a medical student, I basically got in line with the contrary direction that I received during the political unrest. Openly questioning anything could cost you your life. I noted the difference between then and now. I was inquiring about the political process without the threat of elimination hanging over my head. This generates a different thought process – a more judicial and balanced perspective.

I started showing an interest in politics and many of my Ethiopian friends in America noticed. We started having a serious dialogue. My distaste for politics began to evaporate.

Opposition parties in Ethiopia have been allowed since the overthrow of Derg, but they usually have no genuine chance of gaining power. I didn't want to get too excited, but I was especially optimistic when the demonstration by the Coalition for Unity and Democracy Party remained peaceful. Hundreds of thousands walked and watched. It took Ethiopians by surprise, too. First, many Ethiopians assumed that opposition to the government would be met with force and intimidation – as it had in the past. The fact that people were allowed to demonstrate in the streets of the capital without repercussion gave a new surge of enthusiasm to voters. Everyone soon started paying attention to the upcoming multi-party election.

The demonstration also scared the daylights out of the government. It was unaware of how strong the popular sentiment against the government was. Prime Minister Meles Zenawi's (along with his one-party Ethiopian People's Revolutionary Democratic Front [EPRDF]) domination of politics was about to be challenged. When Meles addressed the nation in a televised speech and accused the opposition of fomenting ethnic hatred – even comparing Ethiopia to Rwanda in 1994 – everyone sensed the government was in trouble. They got defensive. The Tigran's planned their own rally for the capital soon after. That demonstration was peaceful too. We were relieved. Although Meles Zenawi had been in power for 14 years – and was hoping to stay in power for his lifetime – at least he was demonstrating restraint and fairness. Two massive political demonstrations – and no violence – this was the beginning. At least, that was our initial impression.

Election Day finally rolled around. Ninety percent of the 25 million Ethiopians eligible to vote came out. Imagine that. Only 58 percent of American's came out in the 2008 presidential election. We were congratulating ourselves on conducting an open political debate – without the accompanying violence. In 2005, 26 Parliamentary seats were being decided – with nearly 35 different parties fighting for them. This was all so encouraging. I was amazed that televised debates on public policy, opposition party access to state-owned media, and peaceful demonstrations were the earmark of this election. We had turned a corner.

Opposition parties competed vigorously (rather than boycott the elections as they had done in the past), and they won 25 of the 26 seats available in Addis, while results for the 547 national parliamentary seats remained unknown.

At least, that's what we understood happened. Observers from the EU, with Ana Gomez as the primary spokesperson, said the closing and counting processes in nearly half of the urban polling stations were suspect, and an unusually high number of ballots were ruled invalid. The situation deteriorated further the following day. Freedom of assembly was banned by the government after the election. Information that was flowing freely before the election now came to a standstill. No one really understood what was going on. People were disgruntled.

On June 8, 2005, people went to the streets again in Addis. To our horror, security forces began to kill those involved. International observers say 36 participants were killed. The government also started to arrest leaders of the opposition. It all felt reminiscent of my youth. Weeks went by without a conclusion to the election. Then months. Hundreds more were arrested. On August 9, amid claims of voting fraud and other egregious irregularities, official results were released: Meles government claimed they had won 296 of 524 national parliamentary seats – more than half, which enabled them to remain in power. I was discouraged – enough to want to do something about it.

The Tigran government was still enjoying unequal privileges while most Ethiopians went unnoticed. The situation grew worse in October. The government placed Hailu Shawl, a leader of one of the many multi-ethnic parties, under house arrest. A CUD demonstration ensued. The security forces turned on them – killing more than 200 peaceful demonstrators in Addis as well as several demonstrators in the countryside. To make matters worse, more than 120 opposition leaders were imprisoned. Demonstrations became commonplace. People were even marching in Washington, D.C., and Ethiopians abroad started to organize.

At about this time, I was invited to participate in a meeting of Concerned Ethiopians. Our goal was to call attention to the situation internationally. In the hope that all Ethiopians – Tigran's, Oromos, Amhara – would devote themselves to the democratic ideal of equal representation, I started attending advisory group meetings in Washington, D.C.

I was talking about the Ethiopian election whenever I could, even at work. I laughed at myself because I used to be the guy who left a room or remained silent whenever a political discussion erupted. Now everything had changed. I was extremely interested in the internal matters of Ethiopia. One night, after a long day at the office, I was speaking to an Ethiopian nurse working for the UN about the situation. She followed the situation as well. Mihret Medhane said, "Guerrilla fighters should be forced to go into a rehabilitation program to civilize them. Someone needs to point out to them that the thug mentality that allowed them to overthrow a government won't work once they get down to the business of governing." She was right, of course. Government by intimidation is counterproductive. Nothing good will come of it except shaky maintenance of the status quo.

But, in this respect, I am sure Ethiopia is not unique. Guerrillas throughout history have been thugs – violent – whether they are the Founding Fathers of Israel, Ireland, or America. Diplomacy skills are not always on the top of the list for nations fighting for independence or a change in government. But aggression is counterproductive when governing. The EPRDF fought the Derg long and hard, and they improved lives for many Ethiopians, but power corrupted them. Thugs need to evolve – and 14 years is too long to embrace intimidation. It was time for a change in Ethiopia.

The international community was key in bringing attention to the situation as it unfolded. Ana Gomez, chief of the European Union Election Observation Mission, remarked a year after the election: "I was fascinated by the law-abiding nature of the people of Ethiopia. And I admire their democratic fervor. Like most Ethiopians in Diaspora,

I'm now not allowed to set foot in Ethiopia for speaking the truth and fulfilling my duty as Chief Observer. We've recognized and openly declared that the EPRDF government deserved credit for organizing an open national debate during the months leading up to the May elections. Despite some shortcomings, the overall process leading to the election was commendable. But elections cannot be reduced to debates and campaigns. They are futile if the people's votes are not properly counted, verified, and certified, and the will of the people duly determine. This is the essence of democracy. In the May elections one year ago, the voice of the Ethiopian people was loud and clear: they wanted to change. But the current rulers of the country did not care to listen, and it is why the democratic will of the people of Ethiopia remains unfulfilled. The Ethiopian people have been, therefore, betrayed by those who continue to govern in their name without their proper mandate."

I agreed with her. While I was grateful that dissent was met without violence, I was deeply disappointed that the voice of the people was ignored. In 2007, I was asked to join the Kinjite International Council, a multi-ethnic organization committed to bringing democracy to Ethiopia. Kinjite means coalition. After all these years of remaining apolitical, I officially became active in Ethiopian politics. Considering what had happened during the election, I felt I had no choice.

When opposition leaders were imprisoned after the election, Hailu Shawel, president of the Coalition for Unity and Democracy in Ethiopia (CUD), and others went on a hunger strike while in Kaliti prison. Different factions of the opposition began to argue – sides were drawn. Many of those imprisoned regretted their decision to boycott the elections. They wanted out, and they blamed Hailu Shawl for leading them astray. After a protracted hunger strike, Hailu Shawl then agreed to sign a document admitting to organizing violent election protests in 2005 and asking for clemency. He was excoriated for signing that document, but 37 political prisoners were released.

After public pressure and the help of Amnesty International, Hailu Shawl was released from prison, but his health was severely compromised. He suffered from severe diabetes. That was one of the reasons he visited the United States.

He was in desperate need of medical attention. So, along with about 20 others from the Kinjite International Council, I greeted him when he arrived at Washington's Reagan National Airport on September 15, 2005. Thousands of Ethiopians came to the airport that day. I also listened to his speech thanking the Ethiopian community in the United States for its efforts to gain his release and the release of other political prisoners. He spoke about the need for unity among the Ethiopian opposition and the importance of avoiding the divide-and-conquer tactics of the ruling regime.

The Council decided to work toward healing the divide between Hailu Shawl and the rest of the opposition leaders. That was our main goal. Members of the Council talked on a regular basis – usually through teleconferencing – to the various factions trying to negotiate some type of rapprochement. We met personally with Hailu Shawl. The Council Chairman was Dr. Tay Woldesemait, who was a political activist imprisoned for seven years by Meles Zenawi, and he was familiar with the dynamics of the situation, but it didn't hurt that he also got help from Amnesty International for his release.

We reminded Hailu that he needed to cooperate with the other factions – while remaining captain of his own ship – for the sake of the country. He insisted on his own position. Solomon Bekele, a businessman who was a member of the committee, openly criticized Hailu during our meeting so that he could correct his position. We continued the discussion, nevertheless. I found it odd that we were defending democratic ideals to an opposition leader who stubbornly held on to his own point of view. I had to keep reminding myself that every Democracy goes through a hard birth. He asked me to contact OLF leader Daud Ibsa, who resided in Asmara, Eritrea, and advise him to coordinate the struggle for democracy. I met Daud a few years earlier along with Dr. Tadesse Ebba who was the chief of the political wing. We discussed in detail while having dinner in a restaurant in Washington D.C, about Oromo politics and the need to coordinate the struggle with other Ethiopians. We discussed that the idea of succeeding is futile. I met with doctor Tadesse several times after that, and he's a very intelligent and accommodating person. I met with him subsequently on several occasions and openly discussed several issues regarding social justice and how to bring change in repressive Ethiopian, Tigrayan dominated politics. He was a brilliant, calm, and adorable person, and unfortunately, he passed away in 2022 after a prolonged illness. I tried to advice Daud Ebsa, regarding national reconciliation but I do not think my advice was appreciated.

My private conversations with Hailu were different. He was much more open-minded and receptive to ideas. He was puzzling at times. I did not always understand why one moment he could be so stubborn, then so enormously brilliant and inclusive, and then, at times, simple and sincere. I fell back on my old views about politicians – basically that they are complicated and difficult to understand. And they can be just as inflexible as a 2-year-old child when an authority figure tells them no.

Regardless of Hailu Shawl's inflexibility, the Council decided to remain committed to him. There was truth to the fact that the opposition was being undermined by the

Ethiopian government. We could not abandon the cause – especially because another election was on the horizon. If we wanted more than 6 percent of the population represented in the Ethiopian government, then we would have to fight for it – in a nonviolent, democratic way.

Prime Minister Meles Zenawi has already warned that government forces would have little tolerance for street protests in the upcoming elections. And the opposition is not united. Birtukan Medakas, a charismatic, 35-year-old former judge who was among those sentenced to prison for life and then pardoned after the 2005 election, is considered a viable force in the 2010 vote. But she was re-arrested in 2007 and ordered to serve out her sentence after saying she stated she had not asked for the pardon scripted by Hailu Shawl in 2005. An alliance of Ethiopian opposition parties threatened to boycott elections scheduled for May 2010 because of the imprisonment of so many opposition leaders. The political situation in Ethiopia was at another crucial turning point.

The International Crisis Group (ICG) began to warn that there was a possibility that a violent eruption of conflict may mar the election scheduled for May 2010 because of rising ethnic tensions and dissent. Thousands of Oromos are in prison. Thousands are in exile scattered all over the world. Ethiopia desperately needs a democratic government – and peaceful coexistence among all its ethnic groups – the time is right for this to happen. But it did not.

Meles Zenawi died on August 20, 2012, while receiving treatment in Belgium at the age fifty-seven. His net worth was reported as $3 billion of stolen money from Ethiopia. This is a public record. I attended his memorial service at Abyssinian church in Harlem, which was organized by the Ethiopian Mission to the United Nations led by Ambassador Tekeda.

Chapter 13: My Teachers, My Patients

Books have always created for me a vital alternate reality. They may be the stuff of the imagined world, but I have always felt a deep connection to them. Often these books are as real to me as my own next-door neighbor. When I used to take those trips into Addis Ababa with my father when I was a child, I always felt exceedingly happy when we stopped at the bookstore and chose a few to take home with us. At night I would crawl into bed with the latest purchase and feel as though I had just uncovered the riches of the world. We all learn from one another. There are many individuals who have impacted our lives by sharing their experiences. Some of them are teachers, and others are my patience. I have so many teachers that share so many profoundly important ideas with me. That's why I consider myself a good teacher because I learned from many others.

If she were alive today, my grandmother would be pleased. Her perseverance in making me sit under that acacia tree to wait for my first tutor – burning all those calories as she chased me around – paid off. By the time I got to high school, I was devouring everything I could get my hands on.

When I was at Haile Selassie I High School in Ambo, after leaving my parent's home, I was homesick, feeling unanchored and alone. That's exactly when I stumbled upon Dale Carnegie's book, How to Win Friends and Influence

People. Odd as it sounds – that an Ethiopian teenager would be deeply enthralled by a best-selling American business book – this book continues to influence me today. I loved it then, and I still love it today.

Carnegie's book – with its simple truths and earnestness – fell perfectly in line with the values I was brought up with in my God-centered home. We were peace-loving, so learning how to get along with others was important in my family. It was a large, extended family, so we had to learn how to compromise, forgive and love unconditionally – or else all hell would break loose. You cannot have 12 children under one roof – as we did in Bako – and do otherwise. Carnegie's book, on the other hand, taught me how to be a friend with the outside world. All those aphorisms in How to Win Friends – "Show respect for the other person's opinion," "Let the other person save face," "Praise every improvement," and "Become genuinely interested in other people" – I took all of these lessons to heart. They made complete sense to me, primarily because they were the values that my father and grandmother, and Tigist lived by daily.

Then I stumbled upon Napoleon Hill's "Philosophy of Achievement," which encouraged me to develop a "definite major purpose." I was immediately attracted to his views on democracy and personal freedom. And amazingly, my life did improve after I read the book. At the ripe old age of

16, I started to become at ease with my fellows, I became more focused and purposeful, and my self-centeredness began to slip away. By the time I was a teenager, I was allowing books to change me for the better.

I made good friends in high school, and when they encouraged me to join their Bible study group at the American Mission, I agreed. I spent long hours immersed in the Bible – during the rainy season (perfect weather for reading) – and again, my life became fuller and richer. The Power of Positive Thinking, by Norman Vincent Peale, also found its way onto my desk at about this time.

These books shaped me and helped me make lifelong friends and mentors. I will not forget how uprooted, and miserable I felt when I first arrived in Ambo. By the time I finished Haile Selassie High I School, by immersing myself in books and showing an interest in my fellows, I was full of hope and optimism. I had a wide circle of friends – many of whom I am still in touch with today.

It is no coincidence that my college life in the capital strained my newfound optimism. Like many of my fellow college students, the political unrest in the capital began to wear me down, tempering my exuberance. My life became dark again. When Emperor Haile Selassie was deposed, I was not prepared for the violence and authoritarianism of the Derg. It was both confusing and threatening. I reached for another writer to help me through it. Bertrand Russell.

By nature, I veer away from controversy. It rarely serves me well. My Oromo tradition has a lot to do with this, I'm sure. Culturally I would prefer to settle disputes and promote harmony. But, in Addis Ababa during the late 70s, none of us could ignore what was going on. Unwillingly I was pulled into a vortex of turmoil and rebellion. I did not want to participate in the violence. I found it repugnant, so I latched on to Russell. His "relative pacifism" – his dismissal from Trinity College and five-month imprisonment for his pacifism during WWI – made an impression on me and validated my own distaste for harm. He condemned The United states' war on Vietnam and was an outspoken proponent of nuclear disarmament. When my friends began to call me Bertrand in college, I was not offended. It was understandable. They were tired of listening to me speak about Russell's views on individual liberty and social justice. My fellows at college would urge me to jump into the fray. I would quote Russell and respond, "Thou shalt not follow a multitude to do evil." They would laugh and good-humoredly blame B.R. again.

But beyond validation, Russell had another profound effect on my life. Although I was sympathetic to the student movement, I remained intellectually detached from it precisely because of Russell's work. I am probably still alive because of Bertrand Russell. Many of my friends at the university were not as lucky.

I had excellent guidance throughout my life, so books were not my only teachers. By the time I arrived at Addis Ababa to pursue my medical studies, Dr. Asrat Woldeyes was already a legend. I was intrigued by him because, like so many of my heroes, he transformed his impoverished childhood (his parents died when he was three years old) and managed to create a fulfilling medical career as a heart surgeon. He was devoted to service and innovation. He had just created the nursing program at Tsehai Hospital – the influx of Ethiopian nurses could not have been more welcome in a country wracked by disease and poverty. When I arrived in Addis Ababa, Dr. Asrat Woldeyes was a member of the Haile Selassie I University faculty of medicine. When I started my clinical training at Tsehai hospital, he gave us excellent bedside teaching sessions.

He was a vocal opponent when the Derg closed the university on March 4, 1975, sending 50,000 students out to the countryside to "help the cause." During the revolution, the Derg asked Asrat Woldeyes to curtail the medical training program at the university – reducing it to three years – so the government could send new doctors to the war fronts sooner. Asrat Woldeyes refused. He said nurses and dressers could be trained in three years – not doctors. His position did not go over well. The Derg sent him to Massawa, a northern warfront, where he administered care to wounded soldiers. My friend Dr. Ambachew Worreta was with him at

Massawa, and he told me a detailed account of work and life at Massawa during that critical period in Ethiopian history.

Fortunately for Ethiopia, he did not perish, and he returned to Addis Ababa to continue to innovate and heal. He never lost his independent voice – even under enormous pressure. When the government of Meles Zenawi tried to divide the nation, Asrat Woldeyes spoke up again. As an Amhara, he was appalled when ethnic divisions began to set the Tigrans against the Amharas and Oromos, and other ethnic groups – he was an Ethiopian first and foremost – and he lambasted the government publicly to cease from its "divide and conquer" tactics. Dr. Asrat was a spokesman for the disenfranchised, and he articulated the majority's thoughts. The regime was determined to silence him, so they planted fake evidence, and Dr. Asrat was imprisoned for five years beginning in 1994. He eventually came to the United States for medical treatment, but by then, his diabetes had progressed so far that he was beyond help. He died at a Philadelphia hospital in 1999. I went to a service in Washington, D.C., to commemorate his life. Many prominent individuals spoke at the service, and laurate Tsegaye Gebremedhin was one of them. When his body was returned to Ethiopia for burial on May 26, tens of thousands of Ethiopians mourned him.

These affronts to liberty were commonplace in Ethiopia – and there were many instances where my teachers were opposed to the prevailing "wisdom" of that government. I admire all of them for their courage – whether it was my pharmacology professor who took an integrated approach to medicine at the expense of his own career or Professor Taye Mekuria, another renowned surgeon, who absconded in the middle of the night to escape Derg repression.

When Professor Taye Mekuria stayed with me during his visits to the United States, he told me about the details of this flight, saying, "What amazed me most was my ability to walk and walk. After an ugly confrontation with the Derg, I decided to leave the country. One night, I drove my car to Dire Daw, leaving my car on the side of the road. I didn't care anything about the car. I just got out and started walking with prearranged escorts. All night long. The next day I hid in the forest and slept, eventually meeting up with a guide later that night. We continued the walk. We would walk all night long and sleep during the day. We walked for another seven days – until I arrived in Djibouti, on the Somali coast, at the United Nations Refugee Organization. I was exhausted, but I was alive. I did not think anyone could walk as far as we did."

I tried to imagine what would have happened if Professor Taye Mekuria had escaped to the United States as originally planned. He finally arrived in Athens, Greek. Instead, what happened is that the Derg discovered his absence and sent one of the doctor's personal friends, Dr Aklok

Habtemichael, to escort him back to the country – probably under threat of life and limb. I could detect bitterness in Taye's voice when he told me about his return to Addis. Perhaps Dr. Taye Mekuria would have had a different – more peaceful – life if he had come to the United States. But he would not have the popularity he had in Ethiopia.

Professor Ede Mariam Tiega established a postgraduate program in the medical school single-handedly. He was a great researcher and educator who impacted the lives of many Ethiopian doctors, including myself. He was exemplary to many doctors. He was not favored by TPLF regime leaders and was mistreated and had to leave the country during the Melese Zenawi era. Even then established a visiting professorship program and had gone back and forth to help medical schools in Ethiopia and, in particular, Gondor medical center. There are so many remarkable Ethiopian doctors and professors who devoted their lives to the progress of medical school. To mention a few professors Demissie Habte, professor Bayou Teklu, professor Nebiat Tefferi, Professor Eyasu Habte Gaber, Professor Tekletsion woldemariam. They are Ethiopian Heroes who were honored by our society-Hakim Workneh and Melaku Beyan society of physicians for international development.

But who can know for sure? What I do know is that I am grateful to many of my professors. Like books, my teachers were instrumental in shaping me.

I have great admiration for teachers, and I have a great admiration for people who open their minds with books. What books and teachers go together is no coincidence. Before I came to the United States, besides the Hale Luya Clinic and my research, I, too, was busy teaching other medical students at the university in Addis. I enjoyed it immensely, and I was determined to follow this path. I believe I would have, except that my first experience at Our Lady of Mercy Medical Center seemed to discourage it. The community at the hospital was not interactive – to say the least – and teaching was not nourished there. But I do think I will continue to teach in private practice; I am, after all, teaching when I give my patients suggestions.

I have been fortunate to have had the opportunity to teach thousands of patients, but what is more important is what they have taught me, especially those I have administered care for several years. EC, a woman from Chile, stayed under my care for more than 15 years. When she retired at the age of 65, she made me promise that I would take care of her for the rest of her life. I agreed. She was a lovely woman, and I admired her. Initially, I wasn't prepared for how everything unfolded, but I will never regret making that promise to her.

EC had crippling arthritis, and it was sometimes difficult to watch her progressively wither, but she was never complaining and was bitter. She told me one day that she knew she would eventually end up in a nursing home, and she asked me to make sure that it was the nursing home I was affiliated with. She didn't have close relatives nearby, so when the time came, I took care of the details. When Alzheimer's set in soon after, and she couldn't remember her own name, she always recognized me. I know in my heart I was a comfort to her – and I felt honored to be able to provide that for her. EC passed away in a few years; I felt a loss as deeply as if she were my own family.

Another patient, RK, I took care of for ten years. He was 87 years old when he first came to see me – full of vitality and alertness. He lived alone, but he always showed up on time for his appointments in a good frame of mind. In his 97th year, he had to begin to rely on a home health aide for assistance. When he missed his appointment one day, the office was surprised and called his home. There was no answer, even though we tried to track him down repeatedly. It was weeks before the home health care aide called the office and told me he was in the hospital. He had lost his way one day when the aide was not there and was brought to a hospital suffering from impaired memory. No one in the hospital knew who to contact. The staff ignored him when RK tried to articulate his wishes, so another doctor was assigned to him – someone he didn't know. He was in terrible shape by the time I found him. It sent chills through me; the thought of losing your way and ending life on that note.

JB, another patient, also inspired me. He was highly educated, with two master's degrees, and financially secure. He had worked very hard all his life – preparing for every eventuality. Although he was single and alone, he had a good retirement plan and health insurance, a comfortable abode, and plenty of extracurricular activities. He seemed like a perfectly well-rounded man. What JB could not plan for, though, was his unexpected physical disability. He became ill after he retired. When he rolled into my office in his wheelchair, he would chide me, saying, "Doctor, you work too hard. Look at me. I always wanted to see the world, but I postponed it, thinking I would do it when I retired. Now, I can't. Don't wait for tomorrow." Seeing people at the end of their lives has been a good reminder to me to cherish every moment. Life passes so quickly. Because of my service to the elderly, I have learned never to postpone what is important. I took JB's suggestion to heart. I decided to see the world. I have endorsed the teaching of Eckhart Tolle in his book entitled THE POWER OF NOW for the rest of my life.

Chapter 14: The Heart of Lightness

The distance between Ethiopia and South Africa is about the same distance as between New York and Los Angeles (approximately 2,500 miles). And just like New York and Los Angles, these two African nations, in many respects, seem worlds apart. The culture, the politics, the landscape, Ethiopian and South Africa followed very different trajectories. Yet I can honestly say the similarities of these two African nations far outweigh the differences. I say this because I am getting better at recognizing similarities.

For so much of my life, I was on the move – sometimes by choice and sometimes by necessity. I used to focus on all the differences of each exotic locale – what made it distinctive and unique – and mentally calculated whether this was a place I could settle and feel at home. Nowadays, I look at each new place, and I see our commonalities.

In October 2009, a small group of physicians from the American College of Physicians embarked on a two-week trip to South Africa. I was impressed with the progress this country had made since 1994 when Apartheid became history. As a doctor, I was primarily interested in the country's medical progress, but I also knew on another level that what happened in South Africa would eventually have an impact on Ethiopia – and I had a strong desire to witness this transformation. We are all connected.

I didn't always feel this way. My life in Ethiopia was one of constant motion. It always seemed that the minute I understood the lay of the land or formed deep relationships with friends, a new event in my life would propel me to another locale. It didn't matter whether the catalyst for change was family matters, education, or war; I just kept moving and adjusting. I suppose this dynamic made me flexible, which is good, but I also felt at times as though I was a leaf blowing in the wind; one strong gust and my life would take a new direction – whether I wanted it to or not.

This can become tiring. At one point, I think it's a good idea to stop reacting to your life and start creating it. That's what happened when I arrived in the United States. I decided to grow some roots. I already knew through my experience in Ethiopia that I could react well in crisis situations. I wanted to see what I would do over the long haul – day by day, year by year. I knew I could win the race, but I wasn't sure I could run the marathon.

Luckily the structure in the States allowed me to get into more training and settle into medical practice – without constant drama, instability, and chaos. I formed strong relationships and developed a good medical practice that made me both financially secure and useful to my fellows. As a result, I grew in my understanding of the human condition – a condition that goes beyond skin color, occupation, preoccupations, and genes. I am fortunate.

While I could attribute this "good luck" to my hard work and intellectual capabilities, I don't think that explains the whole story. I will always be grateful that I was able to thrive and get to know myself in a free, democratic society, but I also must remember that this opportunity signals the beginning, not the end. I must give back what was so freely given to me by God. I have an obligation to help others.

And it was that sense of personal responsibility that put my wheels in gear again. I embarked on trips to South Africa in October and then China in March. I began to think about what I had learned and how I could put it to good use. My two weeks in Africa were key to this understanding.

South Africa is at the southern tip of the continent and has a coastline wrapped by two oceans – the Indian and Atlantic. This was my first visit to South Africa, but I had read a great deal about the progress the country had made since 1994 when Apartheid gave way to free elections, and 19 political parties participated in the electoral process, and almost 20 million votes (as opposed to 3 million in 1989) were cast. I wanted to see that progress for myself. I wanted the same free election process for Ethiopia.

With a group of physicians who are members of American College of Physicians (ACP) on people-to-people mission to South Africa. (At south tip of the continent-Cape of good Hope)

Compared to other African nations, the country has abundant resources, clean air, and a vigorous economy (with a stock exchange ranked in the top 20 of the world). Yet more than 5 million people are infected with HIV-AIDS, and South Africa has the unenviable distinction of having the most cases in the world at that time.

While Nelson Mandela aggressively attacked the epidemic when he was president, he stayed in office only one term, and since then, at least politically, there has been an egregious mismanagement of the crisis – and, as in Ethiopia, a great deal of denial. Government officials either stuck their heads in the sand or advocated combating the disease with roots and garlic as opposed to AZT and Nevirapine.

During my ACP trip, I would examine the crises in South Africa and immediately think of how the situation in Ethiopia was even worse. Ethiopia has the third highest number of AIDS-HIV cases and, to make matters more dangerous, with a population of 80 million at that time, Ethiopia has only 1,200 public service physicians at that time. That translates to one doctor for 61,000 patients. My workload at home in the States – which often keeps me at the office for more than 12 hours a day – suddenly seemed so much more manageable.

During this trip, I felt grateful to be an American citizen. I had created a life beyond my dreams in New York. Like so many other immigrants to America, the road to success was bumpy and challenging, but at least I had a chance to see what I was made of. I saw opportunities, and I did not ignore them. When I was in South Africa, I was reminded that not everyone is as fortunate as we are in America. They have a steeper hill to climb, so now is really the time to share what I have learned – to help others and help themselves.

The two weeks we spent in South Africa were a whirlwind. We visited medical schools, private physicians, and health and research institutions, the Apartheid Museum. We learned about the discrepancy between private and public sectors – where the South African government spends $3.1 billion on medical care for 35 million people while the private sector spends $36.5 billion on medical care for 7 million people (serving only 16 percent of the population). The AIDS-HIV crisis was at the forefront of our discussions, but tuberculosis is also making a strong comeback and causing innumerable difficulties for the population. Without standardization and quality control – measures we take for granted in the State – the country has a rough road in front of it. We found out that, like in Ethiopia, many of the trained healthcare workers leave the country.

Still, South Africa was managing better than other African nations. In comparison to Ethiopia, there is one public service doctor per 12,000 people, and nearly all the children have been immunized against measles and polio. While that may not seem reason enough to be optimistic, in comparison to other countries, we were still encouraged by what we saw. The new government, headed by Jacob Zuma (a controversial leader but popular), has implemented a plan to improve free access to condoms, expand tuberculosis control efforts and distribute free antiretroviral therapy (ART) – and a massive education and mobilization campaign that brings retired health workers back to service. He was also planning to double the number of public health centers. We also visited the school of public health in Pretoria and had a meeting with public health officials and professors. Public health principles are of paramount importance for the well-being of a nation.

On November 2, 2022, history was made in Pretoria. The government of the federal republic of Ethiopia and the Tigray people's Liberation (TPLF) agreed to peacefully resolve the violent conflict that erupted on November 3, 2020, in the Tigray region of Ethiopia in a manner consistent with the Constitution of the Federal Democratic Republic of Ethiopia. This landmark agreement was mediated by His Excellency Moussa Mahamat, chairperson African Union Commission; His Excellency Olusegun Obasanjo, former president of the Federal Republic of Nigeria, and AU High Representative for the Horn of Africa; His Excellency Uhuru Kenyatta, former president of the Republic of Kenya (Panel Member) and Her Excellency Dr. Phumzile Mlambo-Negeuka, former Deputy President of the Republic of South African (Panel Member). This was devastating to Ethiopia as millions were affected. It was a senseless war between brothers and sisters.

During my visit to plateau mountain in Cape Town, there were other groups of visitors behind me speaking in Oromo language, and that surprised me because I knew that many Ethiopians of different ethnic groups must have spread to different regions of Africa, but this is a rare coincidence. I was happy to interact with them, and they were also surprised to find somebody speaking their language. Since my last visit, South Africa has changed a lot politically, socially, and in many other areas.

I came back from my visit to South Africa feeling energized. That's when I began talking to my Ethiopian colleagues about my trip. Like me, many of my colleagues had left their homeland to find peace and prosperity in America, but we were also aware that we still had an obligation to help those we left behind. After a few months of discussion, we decided to build a network to create a link between American and Ethiopian doctors – the Hakim Workneh & Maleku bean Society of Physicians for International Development.

Hakim Workneh is a legend.

Melaku Beyan was the first Ethiopian to receive a medical degree in the United States. Melaku started his medical studies at Ohio State University in 1928, then, a year later, transferred to Howard Medical School in Washington, D.C. In 1926, after being awarded his medical degree from Howard, he returned to Ethiopia and assisted the Ethiopian Red Cross on the Eastern Front during the Italo-Ethiopian War. When Addis was captured by the Italians, he left the country with Emperor Haile Selassie and went to England. When Melaku returned to the States, he continued to campaign vigorously for Ethiopian freedom. He was both a scholar and a top-notch doctor, and at Emperor Selassie's request, he enlisted countless African American professionals to work in Ethiopia. He established a newspaper name "voice of Ethiopia". He established network with activist such Marcus Garvey, Sylvia Pankhurst and many others. Unfortunately, he also was relentless, dying at the age of 40 from pneumonia contracted, as he went door-to-door, passing out pamphlets in the freezing rain to further Ethiopia's cause.

Melaku Beyan was a great inspiration to me. Like the Irish, Italians, Germans, Hispanics, Jews, Poles, and all the other immigrants in the States who came before me, I am deeply proud of my roots. Ethiopia's rich history and culture need to be recognized and given due respect, but we also need to address the country's more critical needs. Famine and disease in Ethiopia will stall any valiant efforts to make progress on other fronts, so a network of support for our fellow doctors and medical practitioners is essential.

Hakim Workneh and Maleku Bayan Society of Physicians – with about 24 members now – met in California in the summer of 2010 to implement this network and extend a hand to our fellows in Ethiopia. We are committed to improving the quality of healthcare in our homeland as well as creating new health centers and training medical personnel. It will be a productive way of giving back.

And I feel more attuned to a healing plan in Ethiopia than a political plan. While I monitored the May 2010 election with great interest, I remained on the sidelines virtually, noting with disappointment all the allegations of voter fraud and harassment. Voice of America's programs in Amharic (the country's primary language) were purposefully jammed by the government. The government diverted funds to its own election coffers. Dissent was smothered whenever and wherever possible.

Election results claim that the EPRDF party won 499 of 536 seats in parliament and, despite claims by New York-based Human Rights Watch, the election will not be challenged. Meles Zenawi is now in his 20th year in power. The good news was that violent outbreaks during the election were sporadic and not widespread. Some critics claim that the administration in Washington is turning a blind eye to the "one-man, one-party dictatorship" and the fraudulent election in Ethiopia because the U.S. depends on the Ethiopian government to keep an eye on Al Qaeda in Somalia. I don't want to venture a guess on this one. All I know is that I will continue to support free elections in Ethiopia – throughout the world, in fact – regardless. Why?

Because free elections are representative, and they work. That has been my experience and the experience of my forebears. It has been verified that Oromo Gada elections were taking place as long as 1000 B.C. We are democratic by nature – proud of it too. And, as far as I'm concerned, I'm convinced that free elections are also one of the best weapons we must use to conquer equity gaps among various populations.

I have had a chance to revisit my experience growing up in Ethiopia while writing this memoir. It has been painful, and it has been liberating. I am happy I was able to acknowledge many people who made a difference in my life – most of whom are no longer alive. I owe them so much. But there were times when summoning these memories during the writing of this memoir that I had to pull myself away from what I was doing – and mourn them. They took a piece of me with them when they died. Ethiopians grieve their loved ones loudly. Writing this memoir gave me a chance to shed all this pent-up anger, frustration, hurt, confusion, and fear that I had managed to bury deep inside my body. I may not have openly displayed my emotions to my community, but I sat still with all the feelings and let them wash over me once and for all.

It is also an Oromo tradition to pass down the stories of our ancestors by word of mouth. As in so many other instances, I have broken with this tradition by writing these words down, but I do it with the utmost respect. I am doing my best to make sense of the violence and political strife that marred my youth so that future generations can avert this senseless loss of life, so they know that closing universities and smothering free speech has dire consequences. There is too much productive work to be done rather than to be sidetracked with horror and suffering.

I sometimes think about Zebib Gayem, my Jehovah's Witness friend who decided not to go to college because of his belief that the world was coming to an end. I don't know how his life turned out, but I wonder what else he put off because of his fears. I am hoping he went back to his village and lived a productive and safe life. That the day the world was supposed to come to an end just came and went without any great commotion. But knowing what I did about the situation in my country back then, I know he had greater worries than the end of the world. No one was really spared all the violence and madness in Ethiopia in the 1970s.

I have concluded that we must not be afraid to keep our minds open and expanding – no matter what.

When I look at my son, who was a teenager when I wrote this memoir, Gamache's fearlessness strikes me because he doesn't recognize how protected he is. He is fortunate to be growing up in the environment he is in – even if he doesn't yet appreciate it. I see him eyeing the world, ready to take on all opponents – big and small. There are times when I think he would be willing to get in the ring with Muhammad Ali to defend his beliefs. I am proud of him (even though, at times, I wish he was just a little bit more afraid of me than he is). He reminds me to stay courageous.

Somewhere between these two worlds of fear and fearlessness, I reside – peacefully and truthfully. It's a good place to be.

Chapter 15: Mindfulness is What Matters Most

Gamachu is my grandfather's name that I gave to my son, who is 25 years old now. Gamachu means joy, and I used this meaning in my attempt to review the journey I made in life. There are ups and downs in life, but I attempted to describe my observations as accurately as possible. Mindfulness is about now and is not about the future nor the past. We learn from the past, but we need to be in the present.

In recent years we have witnessed nerve-racking events or phenomena that transformed the way we live or think about the world. On September 11, 2001, the whole world changed forever as a result of a terrorist attack on the United States mainland. In December 2019, the covid virus was identified in Wuhan, China. The World Health Organization declared the outbreak, a Public Health Emergency of International Concern on 30 January 2020 and as pandemic on March 2020. As a result, the way we live has changed forever. The war in Ukraine is rocking the world in terms of social and economic order and stability of many nations at this moment. There is a lot of violence in many countries, and close to my heart is the ethnic violence in Ethiopia.

When I was brought up in rural Ethiopia, I never heard fictional stories that are told about ethnic differences. Simply put, the narrations and stories of hate between different ethnic groups are unknown to me as a child. Ethnocentrism is the central problem now days. Social and political factors also play a part. When TPLF came to power, it was a master strategy to separate Ethiopians based on ethnicity so that they can create animosity between them. Accordingly, governing would be easy. This was an old tactic used by colonialist powers to control some regions of Africa. Ethnic-based boundaries that were created by TPLF, which was constitutionalized, have resulted in senseless conflicts and bloodshed between people that lived together for centuries. Ordinary Tigray, Oromo, Amhara nor Somali, or any other entity has not benefited from those divisions. Irresponsible politicians, foreign agents, and Nations that desire to control Africa have used every means to destabilize the region by interfering in the internal affairs of Ethiopia. All the mass murders and ethnic violence that was witnessed over the last two years indicate the failure of man.

Global climate change, war, post Covid-19 pandemic, and the crisis has affected millions all over the world.

What is mindfulness within the context of turbulence that I mentioned above?

Mindfulness is the practice of focusing attention on what is happening in the present moment and accepting it without judgement. The phenomena that I mentioned above have been disturbing me a lot over many years. I looked inside myself for insight. I got help from Eckhart Tolle's book

"THE POWER OF NOW: Guide to Spiritual Enlightenment." The guideline helped me to understand my self-better and be an observer of my own thoughts on the process, being more conscious, which is enlightenment. I think his guidance in his book can lead to the deep inner transformation of anyone who practices it.

On October 22, 2022, at 8 AM, I got a phone call from brother Endegena who lives in Helsinki, Finland. After enquiring about my health in the most customary Ethiopian way of exchanging greetings, he mentioned to me that he is deeply disturbed about his partner who is mishandling the two kids they have together. He was very emotional and in tears. Heidi and Endegena are both in the nursing profession and have two kids, a five-year-old girl and a three-year-old boy. He stated that Heidi is not supportive, and he takes care of the kids by himself and more-over the mother is verbally abusive to the kids and slapped one of the kids the other day. He concluded by saying that the situation could get out of control. He sounded to me like he was deeply disturbed by the situation. After listening to him at length, I introduced the idea of mindfulness to him. In order to be free from stress, one must be in the present moment first and foremost. That is the essence of meditation. I mentioned to him Dan Harris's work and A 10% Happier How to Book. I told him that he could download the application from the apple store and follow the instructions. My major advice was to look within himself and be an observer of his own thinking. Repetitive thinking, daydreaming, and negativity that is created within our thought processes can lead to serious anxiety and depression. He was convinced and promised to follow the advice.

A.J. a 38-year-old female patient that I have taken care of in my office for many years. At the peak of Covid-19 pandemic, she got ill and was hospitalized, and fortunately, she survived and came to my office for a follow-up visit. She has been experiencing brain fog, memory problems, and generalized anxiety in addition to breathing difficulty that continued for several weeks. Her anxiety worsened, and she also developed depression. Every time she comes for follow-up, she breaks into tears in spite of the anxiolytic and antidepressant medications that she was taking. The problem was persistent negative thoughts that she would die and was concerned about leaving the baby child behind. I advised her to check out Dan's Ten Percent Happier meditation training application to overcome repetitive thinking. To my great surprise, when she came back for her appointment after one month, I found her transformed and was very happy and jubilant.

Mindfulness can help in conflict resolution. On February 26, 2023, I gave a talk on mindfulness and conflict resolution to a group at St Mary Ethiopian orthodox church in Yonkers, New York. Those individuals were members of the election board and a few others involved in conflict. Election of board members to the church was held in October 2002 and as a result of the process there was some conflict manifested among the church members. I was chosen to the group of elders who could resolve the conflict. Some of the church members are founding members and have been members for more than 30 years The leader of the church is Melake Genet Gezaheng. He is highly educated and dedicated spiritual leader, who also has served as a secretary of the Ethiopian Orthodox church in North America. Other than being a professional he is also a leader and loves his country Ethiopia. He is revered by the members of his church, because of his devotion and dedication to the church. Conflict resolution group was initiated by individuals within the group and I was invited to be part of it. A few individuals within the church had a disagreement during the process of the election of board members in Augusts 2022 that lead to anger, hostility, or animosity. The group of elders that I was part of had a mission to understand the cause of the conflict and resolve it. Dr Wondosen Gebre chaired the group and others included Dr. Getahun Kifle, Ato. Amare woldeKirkos and Ato Genene Zewge During my presentation, I outlined the causes of conflicts in general and that include economic conflict, value related conflict, and conflict for power. There are situations that cannot help to resolve conflicts which includes denial or avoidance, and blaming the other party, using power and influence and manipulative behavior. It is important to know the types of conflicts. The first one is a conflict within oneself and the second one is interpersonal conflict, and the third type of conflict is between a person and a group. Conflict can happen between organizations, or it can be international conflict. Whatever the case might be, it is important to know what brings about to conflicts of any nature. Number one is miscommunication. Secondly, it can be lack of information or misinterpretation of the information, and lastly it could be because of different perspective. Destructive thought patterns, and in ability to regulate our emotions are the reasons why conflicts get escalated. In an attempt to resolve conflict, the main strategy has to be help people to be mindful of their own behaviors. This was what we learned and achieved as a group. This church has been recognized for the harmony and love exercised among its members.

I have struggled for many years to understand the mind. During several years of my medical training and practice, I have learned a lot about the human brain in health and disease. But I have difficulty explaining the mind in view of compulsive thinking that I experience every day. I continue to think of past phenomena, at times very repetitive and annoying. Some of the thoughts come with emotions of anger that could be detrimental. Both negative and positive thoughts can trigger emotion.

On the morning of November 3, 2015, I was returning from my gymnasium work out when my 85D Tesla sedan got out of control as I turned it towards my driveway. It took off and I had to redirect it towards the garage, otherwise it would have gone over deep Clift for my demise. It destroyed my sons Audi vehicle and my Mercedes Benz that was parked in the garage and landed in the basement after breaking through the walls. I cried for God and to this day my survival from that accident is a miracle. The whole debris fell on me and a metal pole that went through the windshield missed me by a few inches. I had only a few scratches. My son was supposed to go to the garage to leave for school just before the incident, but he was in the kitchen when all this happened, otherwise he would not have survived. I came upstairs covered with debris and asked my son to call for an ambulance. He did not know what happened but felt the shock from where he was. My neighborhood friends Peter Obe, Peter Silas, Jeannot Wetzer and Oscar Joseph Dais were about to complete their morning walk and were around my house when this happened. I am a member of the walking club that we established many years ago. That day I opted for swimming and went to the New York Sport club to swim. My friends got immediately involved in rescuing part of the house from falling. When the ambulance arrived, they found that my blood pressure was high. I declined the offer they gave me to go to the hospital because I was feeling alright.

The whole scenario became a repetitive movie in my mind for several months. At times it becomes scaring. When I think of some the major past incidents in my life, I appreciate the value of life now. Past events do not bring remorse in me because they are overshadowed by the power of now. It is my conviction to celebrate today and not to stuck on the past. That is what I call mindfulness.

On March 31, 2023, I was invited to attend a gathering of 2023 World Leaders for Peace &Love held in New York city. I was asked to state my wishes to the world and thus, I made mindfulness my theme. I read my wishes as " I wish the whole world Peace, Love and Prosperity based on mindfulness." At the ceremony, I rung the bell for peace Love and one world, and I was awarded a certificate of Honor in Commemoration of Ringing of the Bell of World Peace and Love signed by Dr Hong, Tao-Tze, President of Federation of World Peace and Love. That made me 499th person to ring the bell. I was selected because of my involvement with a group to fight opioid epidemics a few years ago.

Whenever we face difficulties, it is only natural to push it away and to burry within the subconscious. That involves process of denial and not facing the reality. By doing so we are really running away from the difficulties we are facing. We pretend that nothing wrong has happened and we embrace a different way relating to ourselves and the world.

This means we do not accept the situation. Accepting things as they are is not resignation nor to becoming powerless or helpless. Accepting the situation allows the mind to embrace the true elements of the situation. By accepting the circumstance, we will be able to see the situation clearly and will be aware of the difficulties with all the painful situations and respond to them in most skillful way possible. That is the essence of mindfulness.

Conclusion

My journey in life is a unique experience like other individuals regardless of religion, nationality, or ethnic identity. There are features and experiences that we all share as human beings. The course of events and transformations that take place in the world affects and determines human destiny. That is the trend that my memories revealed.

We are at the defining moment of human civilization. I have endorsed the notion that promotes the power of now as a guiding principle. However, reflecting on the past has enormous benefits in defining the present. Currently, an intense discussion is going on about technological advancements and artificial intelligence. We are all obsessed with those phenomena, and the risks and benefits are also discussed. I started my childhood in darkness when I used candles or kerosene to lighten the darkness to read. When the first electricity generator was planted at Bako during my childhood, and many homes got glowing bulbs, the villagers went frantic. Changes that took place anywhere in the world were shared by multitudes. Henry David Thoreau wrote in his book Walden how he lived a lonely life by building his small home using his labor and outlined the transformations that took place at that time. My life started in a remote village in Ethiopia, and today I am in the greatest city of the world, New York City.

The mysteries of life that were revealed to me through my pursuit of knowledge are humbling and endless. Has humanity reached the climax of "civilization"? Human sufferings that result from violence do not indicate we live in a civilized world. The war in Ukraine and the mass shooting of innocent people in the US or Africa are clear evidence of the failure of man. I have seen books entitled The End of Oil, The End of the war, The End of Diseases, The End of War, etc. Many intellectuals have expressed their concern about social, political, and economic aspects of war and peace pertinent to poor or rich nations. Social media has penetrated the lives of many and are effective in spreading negativity and pessimism all over the world. In most instances, it has become pervasive and destructive. A simple example is to investigate how poor communities in Ethiopia kill each other due to some vague ethnic differences that could be resolved locally. Such fighting creates a vicious cycle of poverty that could be prevented. The ignition forces are currently social media, irresponsible politicians, and money marketing in the business of war creation. Alex De Waal, in his book entitled "The Real Politics of The Horn of Africa" described the role of money, war and business of Power. Recently, I advised a prominent Ethiopian political leader to be an ambassador for peace and national reconciliation, but my advice was in vain because money marketing is the dominant force that controls politics.

Leaders any nation, political leaders, social activist, journalists ext. should advocate for peace and national reconciliation. A true leader is the one who listens and practice mindfulness. The violence that we observe anywhere in the world whether it is in Ukraine, or in the Sudan or anywhere in the world meaningless.

We need mindful leaders, intellectuals, social media managers, journalists, historians, doctors, and many other members of society to work together to bring harmony, peace, and happiness. I believe in the VOICE OF REASON. GAMACHU!! JOY!!

www.ingramcontent.com/pod-product-compliance
Lightning Source LLC
Chambersburg PA
CBHW051545010526
44118CB00022B/2591